SIMONE DE BEAUVOIR

WOMEN OF IDEAS

Series Editor: Liz Stanley
Editorial Board: Cynthia Enloe and Dale Spender

This series consists of short study guides designed to introduce readers to the life, times and work of key women of ideas. The emphasis is very much on the ideas of these women and the political and intellectual circumstances in which their work has been formulated and presented.

The women featured are both contemporary and historical thinkers from a range of disciplines including sociology, economics, psychoanalysis, philosophy, anthropology, history and politics. The series aims to: provide succinct introductions to the ideas of women who have been recognised as major theorists; make the work of major women of ideas accessible to students as well as to the general reader; and appraise and reappraise the work of neglected women of ideas and give them a wider profile.

Each book provides a full bibliography of its subject's writings (where they are easily available) so that readers can continue their study using primary sources.

Books in the series include:

Eleanor Rathbone
Johanna Alberti

Simone de Beauvoir
Mary Evans

Christine Delphy
Stevi Jackson

SIMONE DE BEAUVOIR

Mary Evans

SAGE Publications
London • Thousand Oaks • New Delhi

First published 1996

SAGE Publications Ltd
6 Bonhill Street
London EC2A 4PU

SAGE Publications Inc
2455 Teller Road
Thousand Oaks, CA 91320

SAGE Publications India Pvt Ltd
32, M-Block Market
Greater Kailash – I
New Delhi 110 048

British Library Cataloguing in Publication data

A catalogue record for this book is available
from the British Library.

ISBN 0 8039 8866 4
ISBN 0 8039 8867 2 (pbk)

Library of Congress catalog record available

Typeset by M Rules
Printed in Great Britain by Hartnolls Ltd, Bodmin, Cornwall

For
David, Tom and Jamie

Contents

Preface   *Liz Stanley*   ix

Acknowledgements   xiii

Introduction   1

1   The Making of a Woman   14

2   The Woman and the Words   31

3   The Woman and Women   47

4   The Personal and the Political   66

5   Others   87

6   Reading de Beauvoir   110

Bibliography   128

Index   139

Preface

This series introduces readers to the life, times and work of key 'women of ideas' whose work has influenced people and helped change the times in which they lived. Some people might claim that there are few significant women thinkers. However, a litany of the women whose work is discussed in the first titles to be published gives the lie to this: Simone de Beauvoir, Zora Neale Hurston, Simone Weil, Olive Schreiner, Hannah Arendt, Eleanor Rathbone, Christine Delphy, Adrienne Rich, Audre Lorde, to be followed by Rosa Luxemburg, Melanie Klein, Mary Wollstonecraft, Andrea Dworkin and Catherine MacKinnon, Margaret Mead, Charlotte Perkins Gilman, Helene Cixous, Luce Irigaray and Julia Kristeva, Alexandra Kollontai, and others of a similar stature.

Every reader will want to add their own women of ideas to this list – which proves the point. There *are* major bodies of ideas and theories which women have originated; there *are* significant women thinkers; *but* women's intellectual work, like women's other work, is not taken so seriously nor evaluated so highly as men's. It may be men's perceptions of originality and importance which have shaped the definition and evaluation of women's work, but this does not constitute (nor is there any reason to regard it as) a definitive or universal standard. *Women of Ideas* exists to help change such perceptions, by taking women's past and present production of ideas seriously, and by introducing them to a wide new audience. *Women of Ideas* titles include women whose work is well-known from both the past and the present, and also those unfamiliar to modern readers although renowned among their contemporaries. The aim is to make their work accessible by drawing out of what is a frequently diverse and complex body of writing the central ideas and key themes, not least by locating these in relation to the intellectual, political and personal milieux in which this work originated.

Do women of ideas have 'another voice', one distinctive and different from that of men of ideas? or is this an essentialist claim and are ideas at basis unsexed? Certainly women's ideas are differently positioned with regard to their perception and evaluation. It is still a case of women having to be twice as good to be seen as half as good as men, for the apparatus of knowledge/power is configured in ways which do not readily accord women and their work the same status as that of men. However, this does not necessarily mean either that the ideas produced by women are significantly different in kind or, even if they presently are, that this is anything other than the product of the workings of social systems which systematically differentiate between the sexes, with such differences disappearing in an equal and just society. *Women of Ideas* is, among other things, a means of standing back and taking the longer view on such questions, with the series as a whole constituting one of the means of evaluating the 'difference debates', as its authors explore the contributions made by the particular women of ideas that individual titles focus upon.

Popularly, ideas are treated as the product of 'genius', of individual minds inventing what is startlingly original – and absolutely unique to them. However, within feminist thought a different approach is taken, seeing ideas as social products rather than uniquely individual ones, as collective thoughts albeit uttered in the distinctive voices of particular individuals. Here there is a recognition that ideas have a 'historical moment' when they assume their greatest significance – and that 'significance' is neither transhistorical nor transnational, but is rather temporally and culturally specific, so that the 'great ideas' of one time and place can seem commonplace or ridiculous in others. Here too the cyclical and social nature of the life of ideas is recognised, in which 'new' ideas may in fact be 'old' ones in up-to-date language and expression.

And, perhaps most importantly for the *Women of Ideas* series, there is also a recognition of the frequently *gendered* basis of the judgements of the 'significance' and 'importance' of ideas and bodies of work.

The title of the series is taken from Dale Spender's (1982) *Women of Ideas, and What Men have Done to Them.* 'What men have done to them' is shorthand for a complex process in which bodies of ideas 'vanish', not so much by being deliberately suppressed (although this has happened) as by being trivialised, misrepresented, excluded from the canon of what is deemed good, significant, great. In addition to these gatekeeping processes, there are other broader factors at work. Times change, intellectual fashion changes also. One product of this is the often very different interpretation and understanding of bodies of ideas over time: when looked at from different – unsympathetic – viewpoints, then dramatic shifts in the representation of these can occur. Such shifts in intellectual fashion sometimes occur in their own right, while at other times they are related to wider social, economic and political changes in the world. Wars, the expansion and then contraction of colonialism, revolutions, all have had an effect on what people think, how ideas are interpreted and related to, which ideas are seen as important and which outmoded.

'Women of ideas' of course need not necessarily position themselves as feminists nor prioritise concern with gender. The terms 'feminist' and 'woman' are by no means to be collapsed, but they are not to be treated as binaries either. Some major female thinkers focus on the human condition in order to rethink the nature of reality and thus of 'knowledge'. In doing so they also re-position the nature of ideas. Each of the women featured has produced ideas towards that greater whole which is a more comprehensive rethinking of the nature of knowledge. These women have produced ideas which form bodies of systematic thought, as they have pursued trains of thought over the course of their individual lives. This is not to suggest that such ideas give expression to a 'universal essence' in the way Plato proposed. It is instead to reject rigidly dividing 'realist' from 'idealist' from 'materialist', recognising that aspects of these supposedly categorical distinctions can be brought together to illuminate the extraordinarily complex and fascinating process by which ideas are produced and reproduced in particular intellectual, cultural and historical contexts.

The *Women of Ideas* series is, then, concerned with the 'history of ideas'. It recognises the importance of the 'particular voice' as well as the shared context; it insists on the relevance of the thinker as well as that which is thought. It is concerned with individuals in their relation to wider collectivities and contexts, and it focuses upon the role of particular women of ideas without 'personifying' or individualising the processes by which ideas are shaped, produced, changed. It emphasises that this is a history of *'mentalités collectives'*, recognising the continuum between the everyday and the elite, between 'commonsense' and 'high theory'. Ideas have most meaning in their use, in the way they influence other minds and wider social processes, something which occurs by challenging and changing patterns of understanding. As well as looking at the impact of particular women of ideas, the series brings their work to a wider audience, to encourage a greater understanding of the contribution of these women to the way that we *do* think – and also the way that we perhaps *should* think – about knowledge and the human condition.

Liz Stanley

Acknowledgements

I would like to thank the many people who have helped in the production of this book. In particular, I would like to record my thanks to Carole Davies, and other members of the Secretarial Office in Darwin College at the University of Kent who have typed (and retyped) the manuscript with endless grace. Pat Macpherson read the first draft and provided her usual sympathetic and critical support. I am extremely grateful to her, and to Liz Stanley, for their advice and comments.

Mary Evans

Introduction

When Simone de Beauvoir died in Paris in 1986, the wealth of obituaries almost universally spoke of her as the 'mother' of contemporary feminism and its major twentieth century theoretician. De Beauvoir, it was implied as much as stated, was the mother-figure to generations of women, a symbol of all that they could be, and a powerful demonstration of a life of freedom and autonomy. Around the mother's body, both literally and metaphorically, gathered women from all over the world.

But as de Beauvoir, like all other women, was well aware, the relationship of women with their mothers is never simple. Indeed, identification with the mother is for many women a problematic identification since it involves sharing an identity with a person who may well be socially powerless, and who is, however feminine, not masculine. The emotional and social costs of not being male have become widely understood and documented by contemporary feminism. A generation of feminist writers who have not refused Freud and psychoanalysis as vehemently as de Beauvoir herself did, have been prepared to examine the implications for women of psycho-analytic understanding of the biological differences between the sexes. De Beauvoir's endlessly quoted assertion that women are 'made not born' appears to emphasise the social above the biological, but in juxtaposing the two possibilities she establishes that tension between woman-born and woman-made which is to be an endlessly creative resource in her work.

What follows in these pages is not, and cannot be, given the scope of this essay, either a biography of de Beauvoir or a full discussion of her work. Rather it is an attempt to give the reader an account of de Beauvoir's life, together with some suggestions about the themes and tensions that inform it. Since I first wrote about de Beauvoir (in the early 1980s) feminism has again shifted and developed; unlike some other traditions in Western thought, feminism has remained vital and dynamic, so much so that in a special edition of the journal *Signs* on de Beauvoir's work Mary Dietz noted references to first, second and third generation feminists, all with different relationships to de Beauvoir (1992: 76). What this seemed to be suggesting was that de Beauvoir, introduced here as a mother, had in fact become a grandmother, and that the generation of women to whom she was a mother was fast becoming part of a feminist history, rather than a feminist present. Whether or not de Beauvoir will sit like a 'dead weight' on subsequent generations remains to be seen. At present, there seems good reason to suppose that whether as mother or grandmother, or in whatever relation to feminism, de Beauvoir still occupies a place in what used to be referred to as the canon. Clearly, like all mothers, she has been subject to mixed reviews, but what is notable in many accounts of her life and work is the claim of de Beauvoir as an example. Women write, as they have written of their own mothers, of the 'inspiration' of de Beauvoir, and the strength (particularly strength of purpose) which they have drawn from knowledge of her life and work (see, for example, the women writing in the collection edited by Forster and Sutton, 1989). The construction of de Beauvoir as an autonomous woman-of-letters (a construction in which de Beauvoir was quite as active as anyone else) was one which empowered many women and indicated their determination to lead a life committed to politics and literature.

De Beauvoir as the icon, as well as a maker, of twentieth century feminism, is thus a central figure here. My subject is not one de Beauvoir, but several, all of them inspired by the same actual person and the same social circumstances which inspired de Beauvoir herself. Thus just as 'the other' was a central person in de Beauvoir's work, so the other de Beauvoirs are important here, 'others' who have de Beauvoir's name, but who are often a long way removed from the public person whom de Beauvoir and feminism would like to record. What is raised here, then, is the possibility of the 'bad' mother; to read de Beauvoir as 'the mother' is, in the days of psychoanalytically informed feminism, both far too simple and has far too little allowance for ambiguity and ambivalence. This account will not be an attempt to define the 'real' de Beauvoir, since the existence of such a person is questionable. Rather, what follows is a reading of de Beauvoir and her work; the woman, like her work, is not to be regarded as a stable text. We know that she lived, we know a great deal about her public and private life (and an important function of this essay is also to tell first time readers of de Beauvoir something about the main events of her life) but we know relatively little, particularly from de Beauvoir herself, about the personal dynamic and the experience of the emotional world which made de Beauvoir the person she was to become. As de Beauvoir herself said in *Force in Circumstance*, 'an experience is not a series of facts', and although we need to know the 'facts' about de Beauvoir, we also need to consider those general 'facts' about human beings which help to make us what we become.

De Beauvoir's admitted project in life was to make herself into an independent woman intellectual. Her interpretation of 'independent' was material and intellectual; what it very often was not was *emotionally* independent of Jean-Paul Sartre. Frequently separated from him as she was, she nevertheless remained deeply involved in his life. The nature and pattern of that involvement is discussed in the following pages, an account of de Beauvoir which is informed by my own reading and experience, reading in post-de Beauvoir feminism, in psychoanalysis (and in particular for this study of de Beauvoir, of the psychoanalytic literature on depression) and the experience of motherhood and post-Second World War, Anglo-Saxon culture. De Beauvoir was of the generation of my mother and as such it is impossible not to recognise the similarities between the experiences of middle class women in England and France. De Beauvoir became particular, and more individual than she could have dreamt of, in her childhood ambitions. But she also belonged to a generation of women which was claiming and testing the possibilities of emancipation. France, partly because it remained a predominantly agricultural society for so much longer than England (indeed until well after the Second World War), was slower, in some respects, to allow formal emancipation than England. Nevertheless, particularly in the case of secondary and higher education in France, the absolute central control by the state of secular education made possible the careers of women such as de Beauvoir (and, in the same generation, Simone Weil and Colette Audry). In England, as in France, women born at the beginning of this century were subject to the control of individual patriarchs; equally, both countries were experiencing that process of modernisation which includes the emancipation of women. It was a process which de Beauvoir was to help construct.

The brief account of de Beauvoir's life and work which follows in these pages is written in the context of late twentieth century Europe, a Europe without the political boundaries which dominated much of de Beauvoir's life and a Europe within which women have social freedoms unknown to many women of de Beauvoir's age and generation. Yet for all that, there is still a sense in which 'plus ça change, ça ne change pas'; the very freedoms known to women have often placed them in vulnerable situations, while many normative shifts have benefited men rather more than women. Indeed, looking back on de Beauvoir's life, it is possible to argue that she actually enjoyed considerable freedom and autonomy: she did train for an élite profession, she did live outside conventional society with apparent ease, and to all extents and purposes she lived that life of personal independence which she chose for herself at an early age. Thus to speak of de Beauvoir as belonging to some distant, essentially different, past, in which women were absolutely un-free and subject to patriarchal domination makes a nonsense of her life, and that of other women.

However, what de Beauvoir did help to construct was a self-conscious, theoretical account of the position of women in society. Her contribution, therefore, was to assist in the understanding of the limits of the 'natural' in the ordering of the social world. The great nineteenth century advances in knowledge had been demonstrations that the market economy and human evolution were not works of God, lost in impenetrable clouds, but works and events which were both the product and the possible subject of human understanding. In the early twentieth century Freud was to complete the great triumvirate of Marx, Darwin and Freud, and through his work begin the discussion of the construction of human emotional life. I write, and you read, within the context of the issues and the questions raised by these men. So, of course, did de Beauvoir, and although she often took a critical stance in her work against Marx and Freud, she was nevertheless as much a person of the Western twentieth century as any of her contemporaries. Her central concern was to show that women's social situation could be changed; from a position which initially took issue with the conventional imperatives of bourgeois France, she subsequently moved to a position which demanded change in 'all the social relationships' (most particularly of class and gender) of her given world.

Hence she was to support, in her politics, those governments which seemed to be moving most rapidly towards social transformation. From a position, in the 1930s, of indifference to organised politics, de Beauvoir moved, after 1940, to a clearer identification with the left. Politics became an interest, and for many years of her life a consuming interest at that. But in this account of de Beauvoir's life, what appears to be a radicalisation has also to be read in terms of the ways in which other ideas, besides those of de Beauvoir, developed in Europe after 1945. In the first place – and particularly so from the 1960s onwards – a growing scepticism questioned the idea of progress which so clearly informs de Beauvoir's work, and in particular *The Second Sex*. The major influence in European thought here is Foucault (who always entertained a personal hostility to de Beauvoir), who argued that ideas change, but do not necessarily accord with a model of human progress. His radical deconstruction of the very concept of the Enlightenment *as such* shook the theoretical foundations of writers such as de Beauvoir who believed in development and progress in human ideas. A second – and closely related – shift was the growing articulation of interest in the politics of personal life; for de Beauvoir, politics are seen in terms of government and state structures. Although she is, through her existential inheritance and commitment, an individualist, she nevertheless maintains a model of the relationship of the individual to the social world which is very much that of the classic model of the autonomous citizen who acts in state politics. The 'politics' of interpersonal relations, of communities and of institutions, are largely absent from her world.

Thus reading, and writing about, de Beauvoir in the 1990s offers endless opportunities to illustrate the changes which have occurred between de Beauvoir's world and ours. Reading de Beauvoir for the first time in the late 1960s, her work had then some of the flavour of an account of past times. At that time, I thought that de Beauvoir belonged to my mother's generation (indeed, this was more or less exactly the case). Her preoccupations with dress, the body and codes of manners seemed to belong to a known, but foreign, country. The French families whom I knew in the 1960s were still preoccupied with questions of 'bonne famille' and 'comme il faut', but so were many of their British equivalents; equally, on both sides of the Channel there was a sense of different understanding of the world between generations. De Beauvoir was therefore filed as simply part of an older generation: 'modern' people did not have the same problems.

The compulsive fascination of de Beauvoir – which has now persisted for over twenty years – is not, then, her account of the social world. For me, and for many other women who have written about her, the compulsive fascination lay in the autobiography, and particularly in the relationship with Jean-Paul Sartre. The studious, bookish, de Beauvoir was a resonant figure in my adolescence, since what she appealed to was the adolescent yearning for experience, a yearning largely unaccompanied by actual experience of any kind. That vacuum of adolescent years, when we (or some of us) long for participation in a wider world than that of school and family was filled by the reading of de Beauvoir's own absence of experience and her attempts to engage in Adult Life. So reading about de Beauvoir staying out late, or frequenting dubious Parisian cafés, was a partial substitute for experience. The act of reading about female deviance (or non-conformity) became in itself an act of deviance. Those of us who read de Beauvoir, as well as (rather than exclusively) other, more conventional, fiction saw ourselves, and were seen by others, as engaging in some kind of socialisation for 'being different'.

The nature of 'being different' was as hard to define then as it is now. In some ways the nature of the difference was obvious; de Beauvoir represented a choice about academic and intellectual work, independence and refusal of marriage and maternity. In late adolescence, the difference between this pattern and that of conventional, middle class, southern English, white femininity was apparently clear. Retrospectively, however, the distinction is less clear, since within that supposedly homogeneous class were considerable differences and fault lines whose nature only became clear with adult perception. Equally clear, but again only later, was the recognition that de Beauvoir, in her relationship to Sartre, was more feminine, more traditional and more conventional than the majority of the women we knew or became. My godmother (a form of relationship which in itself is indicative about much of my background) remarked on de Beauvoir, when I was in the sixth form and reading *The Second Sex*, that 'The woman is silly about Sartre'. 'Silly about Sartre' now sounds like a Hollywood musical about de Beauvoir, but the essence of the remark is identical to the comment I was to read years later by Angela Carter, when she asked, 'Why is a nice girl like Simone wasting her time sucking up to a boring old fart like Jean-Paul?' (quoted in Moi, 1994: 253).

There are various comments and answers which exist in reply to this question, including the suggestion that Sartre was not boring to de Beauvoir, or (given what we now know) that de Beauvoir was not a particularly 'nice' girl. Other answers include the thesis that de Beauvoir could not admit she was wrong about Sartre, or that she had invested too much in the relationship to renounce it. More substantially, and much more in the light of what we now perceive about exploitative relationships in general, is the thesis that de Beauvoir was engaged in a relationship with Sartre of such mutual emotional sadism and masochism that neither – and not just de Beauvoir – could leave it. Toril Moi has recently argued the case for the masochism of the relationship; the sadistic element to the partnership is one which will be suggested in these pages.

Hence the sustaining emotional interest of de Beauvoir: of course she wrote fascinating novels and autobiography, but she did so in the context of a relationship which clearly inspired most of her work. To take this comment one step further, I would argue that everything de Beauvoir wrote is a dialogue with Sartre, and thus what she offers is a definite case of the writer whose work has no *internal* boundaries. De Beauvoir obviously internalised ideas about the public and the private (and her autobiography, as the letters published after her death reveal, is full of evasions and silences) yet at the same time what she recognised in the external world, she did not recognise in herself and her internal world. Throughout de Beauvoir's autobiography, most strikingly in *Memoirs of a Dutiful Daughter*, there is a extraordinary sense of a person maintaining a self against the invasion of the world. For de Beauvoir, much of her childhood and adolescence is remembered as a battle against the encroachments of others, particularly her mother. The paradox of this fight to maintain a self is that, once the acceptable other is discovered (in the form of Jean-Paul Sartre), he comes to occupy de Beauvoir's internal world. The 'loss' of Sartre (in the 1930s) was thus a loss which almost destroyed de Beauvoir physically, but allowed her to begin to write. The very paralysis of the pen established by the presence of Sartre *as* the internal world was broken when Sartre became part of an external world.

In de Beauvoir's fiction there are numerous examples of women living lives of misery and constraint because they have made commitments to men which the men concerned wish to end or minimise. These unhappy women are the dependants of men in both a material and an emotional sense: they fail to fulfil their talents and have no independent sense of themselves. We can hypothesise that these women are the fictional projection of everything that de Beauvoir feared about herself: that she would become 'silly' about Sartre in a way which would inhibit her actions, and indeed her very life. Yet she grew up with no model of achieving independence except that of her mother's fierce, Catholic, determination to maintain a relationship (and in her case a marriage) against all odds. Françoise de Beauvoir, as the mother of the 'mother' of twentieth century feminism, bequeathed to her daughter, and implicitly to feminism itself, a problematic, not to say tortuous, relationship to men and masculinity. In the late twentieth century we can say that Françoise had no choice – in that there was no social place for divorced or separated women in bourgeois France of the 1920s or 1930s – but at the same time we have to confront the choices which Simone apparently did have, and could not take. Financially and socially independent of Sartre as she was, she could have changed or ended the relationship; successful in her own right, she could have explored new intellectual and political choices other than those chosen in her days as a student.

But of course she did not, and part of the intriguing nature of de Beauvoir's life and work is her life-long replication of her mother's emotional pattern. Yet at the same time as we observe de Beauvoir demonstrating the same endless ability to work (with real zeal on occasions) to maintain the relationship with Sartre as Françoise de Beauvoir had done with her husband, we also begin to notice that the relationship, however destructive and exploitative, is also rewarding and inspiring. Being with Sartre makes de Beauvoir think, and it made her think in ways which were creative and engaging. Thus to approach the relationship in terms of assumptions about what is good/bad or right/proper about heterosexual relationships risks losing sight of the sustaining dynamic of the partnership: that the couple were bound together by an endless interest in each other's lives. Indeed, for Sartre just as much as de Beauvoir, we can observe a person at work on the creation of the apparently objective and rational out of the complexities and confusions of the irrational.

So being 'silly' about Sartre was, and is, a judgement which still has validity – in that de Beauvoir very often acted like the Sartrean cypher which she was accused of being – but at the same time it loses the intellectual richness which was a feature of the relationship. We can observe, therefore, that in a sense the relationship was actually saved by the intellectual competence of both partners: what could have been yet another emotionally complicated and often destructive relationship was vindicated by the rational powers of the pair. Neither party, towards the end of their lives, could sustain the relationship as it had been: Sartre had to seek and find a quieter and more nurturant presence than that of de Beauvoir, while de Beauvoir turned to more collective relationships. They did not achieve a golden old age, and de Beauvoir pointed out that Sartre's last years were anything but this.

But my first reading of de Beauvoir was not about an old woman, but of one who was – in the 1960s – still young and intellectually active. We grew older together, and as I grew older so the distance, and the fascination, increased. *The Second Sex* and *Memoirs of a Dutiful Daughter* spoke to an adolescent self who wanted to engage in the world, leave a supervised environment and achieve a fully realised heterosexual relationship. What appealed was the vision, in *The Prime of Life*, of intellectual equality; of a man, or men, who would respect female intelligence. The vision faded fast when confronted by British universities in the 1960s. It was apparent that what British male undergraduates appreciated was rather far from the de Beauvoir/Sartre model. Women were in no sense a presence on the campus in those days; feminism had yet to arrive and with it any public discussion of sexual politics. Of course feminism was there, in the sense of a written history and the human presence of the women I had known when growing up: my mother, her friends and colleagues, all of whom had had a higher education and middle class, professional jobs. But it was an implicit feminism, which asserted the potential of women, believed in their competence and their ability, and yet did not, on the whole, challenge the status quo of what education, and the professions were about and for. Ideas about 'male' knowledge, 'patriarchal' culture and institutional and intellectual misogyny were light years away from the seminar rooms of the time.

However, in the 1970s the same feminist energy which was to engage de Beauvoir also engaged me, and at last offered an understanding of what had at times seemed like the fogs of the academy. As clean air became a reality in English cities, so I felt my head clearing as women writers from diverse cultures demonstrated that the culture we were being offered as universal was not, in fact, anything of the kind, but deeply and irretrievably masculine. In Paris in the 1970s de Beauvoir began to read and meet feminists; women turned to her as the author of one of the great books of the feminist canon.

Yet just as rapidly as a canon was established in feminism, it was deconstructed. De Beauvoir consistently dismissed many of the more radical ideas of her compatriots (for example, Irigaray on language) and remained committed to an understanding of the world in which absolute, objective, knowledge was, and is, possible. Her resistance to psychoanalysis persisted, and with it a refusal to admit the motives and the emotional motors which power human action. The de Beauvoir of the early 1930s remained consistent with the de Beauvoir of the 1970s: people could still make 'free' choices, and through those choices construct their lives and those of others. At no time in her written work did any hint of suspicion emerge that she might have replicated patterns in her parents' lives or that the choices she assumed were 'free' were anything but that. The exterior world comprising her independence, her financial security and her literary success were all the armour which demonstrated her difference, as she saw it, from her mother, and her mother's relationship with de Beauvoir's father.

For readers of de Beauvoir, however, the nature of the essential difference between de Beauvoir and her mother is not always so apparent. Thus the issue of 'the mother' and 'the mother of feminism' has its importance here: in our mothers we frequently recognise characteristics we do not care for in ourselves, but with that recognition comes the insight, however unwelcome it may be, that we cannot but share certain experiences with our mothers, since we are, like her, women. De Beauvoir's determination from childhood was to be different from her mother; to refuse not just the literal sameness (which is a commonplace of most generations) but the symbolic sameness as well. De Beauvoir decided that she would stand in a different relationship to the world, and to men, from that of her mother. The paradox, I would argue, is that in this fierce determination to seek difference and separation from the mother, de Beauvoir became the same. Hence my discomfort with constructions and descriptions of de Beauvoir as 'the mother' of feminism: the term, which implies for me a measure of identification between mother and daughter, fits uneasily on a woman whose very emotional intellectual career was organised around the denial of identity with her mother.

But the denial of one mother, in this case Françoise de Beauvoir, was not just the denial of one mother, it was the denial of all mothers: the refusal to contemplate that whether or not women are mothers (and it is, after all, the most common shared experience of the majority of women), they must still confront the possibility of motherhood and the fact of their own mother's existence. De Beauvoir did not ignore the subject of motherhood, but her account of it was generally negative, rather than dismissive or distant. She was, it is apparent from *The Second Sex, against* motherhood. For all that, it was her own mother's death that drew from her the most emotionally vivid prose of her career, and finds her asking, in a tone bordering on the simple-minded, why she is so upset by her mother's death. Her comment is amplified by her remark that she and her mother had little in common.

Thus it is for me when I read that de Beauvoir is 'the mother of feminism' or that she has shown women new ways to live. The common ground possible with de Beauvoir (the outrage at United States foreign policy or the fascination with literature) disappears rapidly and is replaced by the question of exactly what is the nature of the shared world. In individual terms, the question is what do I share with de Beauvoir; in collective terms the question is what do women, in the late twentieth century, share with her. The world in which she grew up, of rigid class divisions and distinctions in an agricultural, imperialist France, has disappeared, but so too, and more importantly, have many of the assumptions of that culture which she shared: beliefs in universalism and progress have long been questioned, just as feminism, and particularly non-Western, non-heterosexual, feminism has brought into question the very models of achievement and emancipation which were once an axiomatic part of feminist assumptions. De Beauvoir's ambition to (literally) 'master' a culture now seems both distant and vaguely absurd: what is this belief, we have to ask, in the possibility of human omnipotence and history? Our values, and interests, have become those of complexity, contradiction and difference: discourses – to use the term of de Beauvoir's compatriot – which demonstrate the multiplicities of power.

For de Beauvoir, however, power was never multiple, it was always cited in single individuals. In the beginning, to paraphrase the New Testament, the word was with her mother; it then rapidly passed to her father and then to Sartre. Here lies, then, a major part of the difficulty in identifying with de Beauvoir: a woman described as a mother, who denied the metaphorical presence of her own mother and for most of her life identified with one man. That mirror to her existence, that lens through which all was filtered (if not seen), remained the core around which all else was organised. However much subsequent critics have tried to reorganise the Sartre/de Beauvoir dynamic (by making de Beauvoir the more creative writer or de Beauvoir a heroine of women's intellectual achievement), the elements of the relationship remain intact. Thus what follows in these pages is an account of de Beauvoir written from a position which rejects the surrogate 'motherhood' of de Beauvoir. She was not, and is not, my mother, and my sense of identity, I can unreservedly state, is derived from an acknowledgement of my literal mother. Moreover, as a mother I further distance myself from de Beauvoir's model of human freedom and separation; my experience suggests that existence is an endless web of connections. The fury and frustration which these connections sometimes provokes is obviously occasionally creative but the rational element of that creativity, I would suggest, should not be to deny the existence of the ties that bind.

In de Beauvoir's life, it is all too striking that she only began to resolve many of the ambiguities in the relationship with Sartre, and moved closer to relationships with women, after the death of her mother. It would appear that until this point in her life she remained locked into the fierce battle of psychic independence from her mother which she could only resolve through an unequivocal commitment to Sartre. Once her mother had died, however, she realised a hitherto unknown degree of emotional freedom. So it might be for feminism, that without clinging to de Beauvoir as the mother/icon of feminism there might be more understanding of the problems of de Beauvoir, both as a writer and as a model of female behaviour. Brecht once wrote that we should pity the land that has need of heroes; so it is with feminism. We should beware those women with whom it is too easy to identify; our identification, and particularly our intellectual identification, needs critical examination in terms of the psychic needs it both expresses and suppresses.

1

The Making of a Woman

Simone de Beauvoir was born, if not a woman then certainly a female, on 9 January 1908. She was the elder daughter of Françoise and Georges de Beauvoir, themselves the children of bourgeois families. De Beauvoir's account of her early life (in the first volume of her autobiography, *Memoirs of a Dutiful Daughter*) conveys to us something of the social exclusivity and relative privilege of this world (de Beauvoir, 1959)[1]. The de Beauvoirs, despite the financial problems of Françoise de Beauvoir's family and the uncertainty of Georges de Beauvoir's professional and earning competence, lived as if their world was solid and endlessly sustainable. The divisions between the classes in early twentieth century France were sufficiently rigid for the bourgeoisie to suppose that their social position and their social authority were absolute. Certainly, much of *Memoirs of a Dutiful Daughter* is about social division and caste-like patterns of social segregation. Simone and her younger sister Hélène were endlessly watched to make sure that they did not play with 'undesirable' children; their clothing, their manners, their early education and their social contacts were rigorously policed to ensure that there was no contamination through contact with the socially unacceptable.

The irony of this exercise was that it was eventually Simone de

Beauvoir who would become socially undesirable to her own class, and an outsider to the world in which she was born. This transformation has partly occurred at the end of *Memoirs of a Dutiful Daughter*, by which time Simone has graduated in philosophy from the Sorbonne and has turned her back on the values and assumptions of her parents' class. But in the account of this emancipation de Beauvoir contrasts her fate with that of her friend and contemporary Elisabeth le Coin (referred to as 'ZaZa' in de Beauvoir's autobiographies). Dead from an undiagnosed illness in her teens, Elisabeth becomes the first of de Beauvoir's 'others', the person whose fate is different from her own and who remains trapped (and in de Beauvoir's view killed) by bourgeois codes.

Yet in escaping from what de Beauvoir suggests to us are iron and inflexible laws of social behaviour, she also portrays her own sense of powerlessness to renegotiate the boundaries in which she lived. The constraints which she experienced were in no sense not real, but de Beauvoir's perception – that all the constraints were external – has to be tempered by the knowledge of internal constraints. That is, that de Beauvoir, far from rejecting her parents' world, had so much internalised it that she identified it as a monolithic source of authority when it was actually far less rigorous. The example of her own father – who lived out his own life far removed from anything that was publicly acceptable – might have suggested that the bourgeois world is capable of sustaining considerable diversity of difference. A clever, well read, man, Georges evidently found the life of a conventional *bourgeois gentilhomme* unpalatable and as disappointment and conflict in his marriage, together with financial hardship and professional failure, took their toll he turned more and more to a private life lived in cafés. His home, once the place in which he had entertained his friends and lived a public, social life, now became the private place from which he was frequently absent and to which he would return late at night and frequently drunk. 'Things went wrong in lots of ways' is how de Beauvoir was later to describe her childhood, and how they went wrong is that the family became poor and Georges and Françoise found their relationship ever more difficult to maintain.

For the children growing up in this home, the world was one of complex contrasts, evasions and constraint. Simone de Beauvoir and her sister were born into *Belle Epoque* plenty and the experience *and* expectation of ease and prosperity. The sisters' parents were well enough materially provided for to pay for private education (and state, secular, education would have been out of the question for Simone's pious Catholic mother) – and to consider themselves as part of a social élite. But as the First World War destroyed the financial basis of the de Beauvoir world, so the world itself developed deep fault lines. The elegant flat in which de Beauvoir was born, and in which she lived her early childhood, was substituted for another, much smaller and less grand, apartment. More critical still, in terms of the internal organisation of the family, was the enforced departure of the live-in maid-of-all-work, Louise. Françoise de Beauvoir, once able to assign all domestic work, and much childcare, to someone else, now found herself cooking and shopping, carrying water up endless flights of steps, emptying slop buckets and generally being a housewife in what we would now in the West regard as primitive conditions. The housework which Simone and Hélène saw their mother perform was menial, hard work. Inevitably, both sisters were well aware that it was Françoise and not Georges who took over this work, and that this was regarded uncritically. Women in France in 1920 did not question the assumption that domestic work was their responsibility. What Françoise clearly did do was question Georges' competence as a provider; masculinity, Simone must have learned, is expected to rest on a foundation of competence at provision.

So in the first 10 years of de Beauvoir's life she lived through a series of social experiences and social constructions of masculinity and femininity. The mother and father of early childhood were largely at one with bourgeois expectations; the father provided and knew about the public world while the mother offered private nurturance and supervised and decorated the domestic space. Financial hardship virtually abolished the material competence of the father, while the mother had no choice except to develop domestic skills. At the same time as this was going on chez de Beauvoir, the households of Simone's relatives and friends remained consistently prosperous and well provided for. Thus what had begun as an 'ordinary' bourgeois life became, quite rapidly, an extraordinary bourgeois life, in that it was largely family and social connections, and values and aspirations that kept the de Beauvoirs among the bourgeoisie. They became, as a family, what the English describe as the 'genteel poor'. The problem, however, about this description of the de Beauvoirs was that while Françoise did retreat into Catholicism and an increasing adherence to rigid rules about manners and behaviour as the family became poorer, Georges became markedly less well behaved. Thus to picture the family as living out a Cranford-like existence of polite scrimping and saving misrepresents the actual reality of the household, in which Françoise stormed and shouted about her lot and Georges spent little time at home.

In these difficult circumstances, it might have been the case that Simone and Hélène would have identified with their mother, sympathised with her situation and made a common, female, cause against the world. That this was not the case (and in fact the reverse seems to have been true, particularly for Simone, in that she turned away from her mother to her father) is understandable in terms of three factors. First, Françoise, however much she vented her rage, anxiety and exhaustion on her husband, also directed a great deal of it at her daughters. Like millions of other women, she found that being a 'good' mother was considerably easier when provided with a sufficient income and a reliable husband. The absence of both did nothing for Françoise's temper, and Simone and Hélène were frequently the target of their mother's anger. Thus the daughters became alienated from their mother, whose very presence they began to regard as an irritant and a threat to their growing sense of autonomy. The second, and closely linked, reason for de Beauvoir to turn away from identification with her mother was religion, or more specifically her mother's rigid Catholicism. The piety of Françoise was in stark contrast to Georges' consistent and articulate refusal of religion. Throughout his life (and indeed on his death bed) he refused any contact with the Catholic church, and although he was prepared to allow his daughters to be educated in Catholic schools, he was equally prepared to encompass Simone's enrolment at the Sorbonne and her own avowed rejection of Catholicism.

The issue of religion was not, however, simply one of different beliefs within one family. Other families contain such differences, without the children adopting rigid positions of one kind or another. In the de Beauvoir household what seems to have been at issue was religion as an organising morality, not just as a matter of belief. In a passage in her biography of Simone de Beauvoir, Deidre Bair describes the way in which Françoise de Beauvoir made religion a living reality:

> As her daughters grew to young womanhood, Françoise became an even more intrusive presence in their lives. Her work, as she perceived it, became even more time-consuming and demanding. The never-ending household routine was compounded by all the new things they were exposed to in their daily travels to and from school, as well as by what they learned there. Françoise became militantly alert to make sure they were not corrupted. Now, if characters in a book were in love but not married, she banned the book; if there were parts she disapproved of, she clipped those pages together and her daughters were not allowed to read them. She made the three daily trips to school on the Metro or the bus until they cried that they were too big for such supervision, but she continued to watch them like the proverbial hawk everywhere they went outside the apartment long after she could do nothing to control their movements or companions. They even caught her far too often listening outside their bedroom door on the infrequent occasions they had time to idle away in daydreams and conversation. She was ubiquitous and, in consequence, an irritant. (Bair, 1990: 62)

This universal policing of her daughters had the obvious and inevitable effect of producing in them resentment at their mother, and a pattern of minor deceit about their activities. These adolescents could not rebel in a way which might be more familiar in the 1980s and 1990s, but what they did was to develop an indomitable determination to maintain their own values and interests in the face of opposition. Simone, it is quite apparent, simply went to ground in these adolescent years and learned a pattern of steely single-mindedness. She decided she would read philosophy, so she read philosophy. When she then decided to take the highly competitive examination to allow her to teach the subject in state secondary higher education, she also did that. The blinkered and narrow existence forced on the de Beauvoir sisters by the family's poverty and the mother's obsessive fear of moral pollution was entirely functional for Simone; in a life of no distractions, she was able to pursue her own goals of scholastic success. The mundane adolescent rebellion of other teenage girls about clothes, boyfriends and social life was channelled by de Beauvoir into an obsession with academic work.

So de Beauvoir's mother passed on to her daughter little in terms of explicit agreement on moral values. Precisely because Françoise de Beauvoir's standards and understanding were so narrow and so limited, it was simple for her daughter to turn her back on them. Her mother's thoughts could be identified, without great intellectual prowess, as bigoted and ignorant. With a father who enthusiastically embraced literature and the arts, and was both literally and metaphorically prepared to be a citizen of a cosmopolitan and urban world, Simone had an alternative model of understanding. Because she was a girl, and a girl of a *bon bourgeois* family, she was not allowed access to this world, but as her father's daughter she was left in no doubt that this world existed.

Thus her mother's behaviour and values were such that between mother and daughter (and to a lesser extent mother and daughters) there developed a chasm of hostility, dislike and frustration. The personal consequences of this estrangement are manifest in de Beauvoir's autobiography and her fiction; she writes seldom about her living mother and peoples her fiction with few mothers. Nevertheless, her mother's death gives rise to *A Very Easy Death* (1965b), which is an anguished testament both to the life and the death of her mother. Part of growing up in the de Beauvoir household inevitably produced the dualism, and the sense of sharp difference between women and men, which is a characteristic of de Beauvoir's work. Mother and father were different, not just in the obvious ways of daily tasks and preoccupations, but in attitudes to the world and its values. What had once been a conventionally satisfactory, and conventionally organised, marriage, collapsed into two very different lives as circumstances changed. But we are also told about the evident sexual satisfaction of the early days of the marriage. Indeed, much of the early part of *Memoirs of a Dutiful Daughter* speaks of physical pleasure; of sexual and erotic pleasure between the parents, and of the child's pleasure at the warmth of physical contacts and the delights of feeding. The body (both collective and individual) in the de Beauvoir home is well provided for in these early days.

But then the world changes. We know that the parents start to quarrel, the food becomes scarcer and poor, the clothes ugly and uncomfortable and the physical surroundings unpleasant. Narcissism is hardly encouraged in this world, let alone gratification. Nevertheless, the one person who remains able to gratify himself – through casual sexual encounters, drink and café society – is Georges de Beauvoir. While mother and daughters stay at the not-very-nice home, Georges continues to seek, and find, sensual satisfaction. So in the first of her many silences and evasions, de Beauvoir does not elaborate on the costs to her mother of this pattern of behaviour, except to say (more than once) that her mother was trapped in a rigid moral code which dictated her behaviour.

Throughout her account of her childhood and adolescence, de Beauvoir speaks frequently of her outbursts of temper, the rows with her parents, the tears and tribulations which she endured. It is equally apparent from *Memoirs of a Dutiful Daughter* that for a considerable amount of her early life de Beauvoir felt both lonely and on trial. When she did form friendships they became (as with her cousin Jacques and friend ZaZa) all-encompassing and passionate. The early close relationships with her parents shifted in her adolescence to relationships in which she manifestly tried to please. First, she tried to please her mother by believing in God (and, for example, attacking herself with a pumice stone in order to mortify the flesh and produce an appropriately 'spiritual' response). Second, she tried to please her father by success at school, but although he was prepared to acknowledge her brilliance, any pleasure in that achievement was rapidly taken away by remarks about ugly blue-stockings or the greater physical attractiveness of her sister. In both attempts and endeavours, the successes of Simone became aborted by the sense of failure of the parents. When Simone professed (despite earnest attempts) to have no belief in God, this became her mother's failure. Equally, the very fact of Simone's success at school was viewed by her father as a demonstration of his failure: if he had been a successful man, his daughters would have had a dowry, the expectation of acceptable bourgeois marriages and no need to swot away at exams. Little wonder that Simone was to write of her plans to be a teacher, 'If at one time I had dreamed of being a teacher it was because I wanted *to be a law* unto myself' (de Beauvoir, 1959: 142).

The italics here are mine, and used to emphasise the young (and older) Simone's need for a coherent universe. Manifestly, her home did not provide her with one. Her assumption that she could please her father by scholastic success was rapidly undermined by his negative remarks about her appearance and his praise for the physical charms of his younger daughter. Her childhood picture of her parents as a loving couple was daily disallowed in her adolescence by the rift between them. In contrast to the parents of many of her friends, Simone found herself living in a deeply unintegrated household, in which the two sources of initial integration of husband and wife (material prosperity and mutual sexual desire) had long disappeared. Inevitably, Simone compared her home with that of her friend ZaZa. While the le Coins lived in a state of educated, conservative, Catholic harmony, the de Beauvoirs lived in a state of dissent and disharmony. Further, the very presence of nine children in the le Coin household was demonstration of the continuing sexual relationship between the le Coin parents. To be a child of only two was something of a rarity in France (indeed Europe) in the early 1920s, and since artificial contraception of any kind was illegal in France at the time, we can conjecture that the de Beauvoir marriage had probably become sexually inactive.

To grow up in such a marriage may, or may not, have a lasting effect on children. What can be said, however, in terms of de Beauvoir's own sexuality and sexual history, is that, even by her own account, her sexual development and her relationship to her body was not a happy one. In *Memoirs* she writes of her gawkiness, her sense of her unattractiveness and her physical discomfort as an adolescent. In passage after passage she tells us about her awful clothes (so awful in fact that she was often the subject of other people's jokes and unkind remarks) and then, in one of her breathtaking denials, assures us that she was 'not at all vain'. Longing to be attractive, and to be thought attractive, the adolescent Simone took refuge in literature and morbid depression. Her own sense of self had to confront a daily litany from her parents that she was the 'wrong' sex: ' "What a pity Simone wasn't a boy: She could have gone to the Polytechnic!" I often heard my parents giving vent to this complaint' (de Beauvoir, 1959: 177). As it was, their daughter had an almost freak-like ability to overcome the disability of inadequate teaching at a Catholic school and emerge as one of the outstanding pupils in national competitive examinations.

When Simone de Beauvoir finally passed her formal examination in philosophy she was placed second, as every reader of her autobiography knows, to Jean-Paul Sartre. As the note on the author in the Penguin edition of the autobiography says, Jean-Paul Sartre became 'her firm friend'. The description is as rich in ambiguities as was the relationship between these two people. De Beauvoir was to remain firm in her commitment to her relationship with Sartre to the end of his life, and for the remainder of hers. But whether or not Sartre gave the relationship the same commitment remains unknown. Of the manifest inequalities in the relationship, one remains striking: it is de Beauvoir and not Sartre who is the historian of the 'friendship'. Sartre maintained an absolute silence on the matter, and although some of his letters to de Beauvoir have been published, they remain the sole testament to a relationship which lasted for over fifty years.

When Sartre's letters to de Beauvoir were posthumously published (in 1983), the English title was *Witness to My Life* (Sartre, 1992b). The title is drawn from remarks Sartre made in 1974 when, in an interview with de Beauvoir, Sartre commented that his letters were 'the transcription of immediate life ... In effect my letters were a witness to my life' (de Beauvoir, 1984: 177). The use of the word witness here is evocative of de Beauvoir's own comment about becoming 'a law unto myself'. Both these people, frequently regarded as pariahs by their own society, were nevertheless entirely integrated into its central, modernist, belief: that there are universal, general laws and the world, through properly developed and understood 'laws', can be rendered coherent. To understand de Beauvoir, and indeed Sartre, it is essential to situate her not just in France (and urban, cosmopolitan France at that) but in the intellectual climate of European modernity. We now write about de Beauvoir from the standpoint of late twentieth century postmodernity; our understanding of the world has been fractured and indeed deconstructed in ways which Sartre and de Beauvoir never had to confront. For them, in 1929, celebrating their triumph as graduates of a rigorous examination system, the bourgeois order had to be questioned, even remade, but in general and universalistic ways.

The first encounters between Sartre and de Beauvoir were negotiated through intellectual concerns. While a student at the Sorbonne, de Beauvoir had been courted by other young men, who had praised both her looks and her academic competence. Never deemed sexually desirable by her father, de Beauvoir nevertheless discovered that other men found her attractive and even sexually desirable. The elegance which was to become occasionally apparent in her later life was emerging, and as the distance between herself and her family increased, the sense of inadequacy and depression was also disappearing. Men were now affirming her as both a woman and as an intellect; she was doubly attractive, it is clear, both because she was objectively attractive and because she was a very rare person – a woman in French higher education in the 1920s. Her spirits lift as her fellow male students praise her choice of hat or her looks. In this new world she does not have to confront the problems of relationships with women or indeed of defining her own sexuality. Since there are virtually no women in this new intellectual world, there is little scope for female friendship within its boundaries. Equally, the very existence of a woman in such a world was sufficient to identify the woman in sexually positive terms. It is not until the second volume of de Beauvoir's autobiography, *The Prime of Life*, that women – as a group, a category or indeed a sex – reappear (1962a). When they do, de Beauvoir was to write about women with something of the surprise and enthusiasm of a Columbus:

> Now, suddenly, I met a large number of women over forty who, in differing circumstances and with various degrees of success, had all undergone one identical experience: they had lived as 'dependent persons'. Because I was a writer, and in a situation very different from theirs – also, I think, because I was a good listener – they told me a good deal; I began to take stock of the difficulties, deceptive advantages, traps and manifold obstacles that most women encounter on their path. I also felt how much they were both diminished and enriched by this experience. The problem did not concern me directly, and as yet I attributed comparatively little importance to it; but my interest had been aroused. (1962a: 572)

De Beauvoir wrote this passage (in 1960) about herself and her reactions to the world in 1945. *The Prime of Life* is dedicated to Sartre and it is Sartre who dominates the work. The relationship

which had begun at the Sorbonne in 1929 had survived physical
separation and multiple infidelities. In the years between 1929 and
1945, both parties had become writers (although the years of their
global fame were yet to come) and they had established themselves as leading intellectuals. In fact, they had both realised their
ambitions: to write (and to be writers in the full professional sense)
and to live lives unfettered by ordinary domestic and personal concerns. They had lived (and continued to live for some time
post-1945) in hotels and ate in cafés. Yet for all this apparent
bohemianism, the couple maintained social lives of great consis-
tency and stability. Both de Beauvoir and Sartre were in close
contact with their families (particularly Sartre with his mother)
and the geographical locus of their lives remained a small area of
Paris around the Boulevard Montparnasse. They lived in, and to a
certain extent with, the world into which they had been born. As a
couple, Sartre and de Beauvoir travelled widely throughout Europe
in the 1930s, but the essential parameters of their lives were
constant: school teaching to provide a living and travels in the
school holidays.

This ordered existence was disturbed emotionally in the 1930s
by the three-sided relationship between Sartre, a student named
Olga Kosakiewicz and de Beauvoir. The situation eventually made
de Beauvoir seriously ill, although it was also to provide the raw
material for her first and perhaps most powerful novel, *She Came to
Stay* (1966). At the beginning of their relationship de Beauvoir and
Sartre had made a pledge of absolute commitment, but not
absolute fidelity. When Sartre had relationships with 'other'
women, de Beauvoir had (by her own account) successfully negotiated them. Olga was a different case, and the fury and jealousy of
de Beauvoir's feelings were made apparent in *She Came to Stay*, in
which the de Beauvoir character finally kills her rival. What made
Olga so different is, of course, the key question. Whatever the
answer, she provided de Beauvoir with the essential motivation to
write fiction – a motivation which had previously been lacking and
which had led Sartre to accuse de Beauvoir of becoming a 'female
introvert' (1962a: 61).

The accusation was a moment of crisis in the relationship
between Sartre and de Beauvoir. The retelling of the conversation

prompts de Beauvoir to make two points. First she translates and develops Sartre's 'female introvert' into 'a mere housewife'. Second, she turns upon herself, and not Sartre, in fury: 'I was furious *with myself* for disappointing him in this way' (1962a: 61). Once again, it would appear, de Beauvoir had failed to please the significant male other in her life, and because of that she should expect to be punished. The form that de Beauvoir's self-inflicted punishment takes is a four page tirade against sexual need and sexual pleasure. Starting with an apparently frank avowal of the sexual fulfilment of the early days of her relationship with Sartre, she moves to a discussion of the sexual needs that she now has. But these sexual needs are described in a language which suggests that a sexual life is also a life of enslavement. De Beauvoir speaks of being a 'victim' to her newly awakened sense of sexual desire and of the 'shameful disease' of desire that invades her body. She writes of her feelings, and their implications for her relationship with Sartre:

> I was forced to admit a truth that I had been doing my best to conceal ever since adolescence: my physical appetites were greater than I wanted them to be. In the feverish caresses of love-making that bound me to the man of choice I could discern the movements of my heart, my freedom as an individual. But that mood of a solitary, languorous excitement cried out for anyone, regardless ... I said nothing about these *shameful* incidents. Now that I had embarked on our policy of absolute frankness, this reticence was, I felt, a kind of touchstone. If I dared not confess such things, it was because they were *by definition unavowable.* By driving me to such secrecy my body became a stumbling block rather than a bond of union between us, and I felt a burning resentment. (1962a: 63)

The italics in this passage are mine, and not de Beauvoir's, and my emphasis is derived from an understanding of the body, desire and sexuality which has been formed within a context of the acceptance (at least formally) of female sexual desire, and the existence, within women, of sexual desire which is independent of a particular person. The sense of secrecy, fear and self-loathing in which de Beauvoir discusses her awakened sexuality is one which, while far from being absent among contemporary women, would now be regarded as problematic rather than inevitable.

The expectation that female sexuality should only be aroused by a particular man was (and no doubt still is) a view which de Beauvoir had inherited from her father and her mother. Indeed, the sexual relationship with Sartre is defined and defended by de Beauvoir in terms of its demonstration of her 'freedom as an individual'; that is, that sexual activity is legitimated through the 'choice' of a particular person. Again, we see in de Beauvoir a need for legitimation and permission: sex with Sartre is acceptable precisely because it is that. The shift in de Beauvoir's work, and world, towards sex-in-itself, comes after the trio episode and at the point where de Beauvoir conspicuously identifies Sartre's sexual liaisons as inferior to her relationship with him.

This sense of containment, of sexual relationships being precisely that and not necessarily involving emotional, let alone social and intellectual, commitment, was part of the transformation of the de Beauvoir/Sartre relationship which occurred after the complex relationship with Olga, a relationship in which de Beauvoir had played an active part as both spectator, partner (to both others) and commentator. Prior to that incident, de Beauvoir had pledged that theirs would be a permanent, but not exclusive, relationship. De Beauvoir had agreed to Sartre's terms of 'contingent affairs' and, by her own account, accepted these affairs when they arose. But Olga clearly aroused deeper passions, and from that point a sense of separation arose between de Beauvoir and Sartre which was to have long-term implications for her. For Sartre, the relationship involved what one of his biographers, Annie Cohen-Solal, has described as the last stage in the fall of Sartre's narcissism (1987: 108). Convinced that he could achieve great status as a writer and philosopher as a young man and order the world by rational will, Sartre had found (like de Beauvoir) that our wishes do not necessarily coincide with the world's inclination to grant them. For both, their twenties were a time of accommodation. Beset by a sense of failure, Sartre fell passionately in love with Olga, who seemed to offer him an escape from the intellectual, rational world which he had constructed with de Beauvoir. 'Passion and madness' are the words which Sartre was to use to describe those years.

From those years emerged de Beauvoir's *She Came to Stay* and Sartre's *Le Mur* (1939) and the first volume of the *Roads to*

Freedom, L'Age de Raison (The Age of Reason) (1945). The emotional life was rapidly turned into literature and used as a resource. But through those experiences Sartre and de Beauvoir had become a different kind of couple, and a couple in which intellectual life constituted the essential bond. The letters exchanged between them gave each details of their emotional and sexual encounters with other people, all the while constructing the descriptions of these events within a theoretical model of existential conjecture. At the same time, what is striking is the emotional form which the letters take. Both invariably begin their letters with protestations of love; having established that point, they go on to describe their activities with others. Thus reassurance to the other party comes first, closely followed by evidence of independent life outside the relationship. The other striking characteristics of the letters are the perpetual use of 'little' in the exchanges and de Beauvoir's self-description as 'charming'. Thus in a letter to Sartre in 1939 de Beauvoir writes: 'O yourself, I love you so, love you in the real sense of the word. I have a passionate need for you. Oh little shadow, do become flesh and blood – I so need your little arms around me!' (1991: 143); and she signs herself, as often, 'Your charming Beaver'.

Writing to de Beauvoir at exactly the same date, Sartre addresses the letter (as he does to the other woman he is currently corresponding with) to 'my darling' or 'my love' and concludes by thanking de Beauvoir for her 'little' letters. Capable of expressing passionate, unquestioning love for de Beauvoir, he is equally capable of immediately qualifying this sentiment. For example: 'Everything good that I am is because of you. I love you. The Moon Woman is perhaps right in saying that I over-estimate you, my little flower. I love you passionately' (Sartre, 1992b: 301). An ending, if ever there was one, replete with ambiguity. But that ending – or that form – was to continue to dominate the relationship for the remainder of their lives. At the end of the Second World War de Beauvoir and Sartre emerged as nationally, and subsequently internationally, known figures in French culture. Initially famous as the founders of existentialism, their fame was to involve the authorship of numerous novels, philosophical works, and in de Beauvoir's case studies of women – *The Second Sex* – and a lengthy four volume autobiography. Sartre was to dominate that autobiography, and the man without whom de Beauvoir confessed to feeling 'lost' and 'disinterested' is omnipresent in her work. But as well as considerable individual fame, de Beauvoir and Sartre became famous as a couple, and as a couple in two senses. First, they are famous because of their joint political activism (dating from the Second World War) which took the form of radical left wing politics. While never members of any political party, both became involved in opposition to the colonial and imperial policies first of France and subsequently the United States. The first and most furious political struggle of which they were part was the decolonization of Algeria. De Beauvoir and Sartre were fervently opposed to the French government's attempts to maintain French authority over Algeria, and in doing so became the targets of those extreme right-wing elements who wished to continue direct French rule. Later political campaigns involved opposition to United States policy in Vietnam, and support to Israel in the politics of the Middle East. At one with Sartre in these campaigns, and indeed his frequent travelling companion on journeys to embattled and/or socialist societies, from the early 1970s de Beauvoir increasingly became involved in campaigns of her own – campaigns associated with feminism and her growing association, from this period, with explicitly feminist activity.

In middle, and later life, the couple endured. They became known, not just for their joint and individual work, but as a legendary couple, and one which represented 'intellectual life'. Never occupying a shared domestic space, or owning common property or having children, de Beauvoir and Sartre came to represent a couple who lived outside the general conventions of what is expected of 'couples', whether heterosexual or homosexual. Yet for all their avoidance of the conventional organisation of personal life, it is evident from their letters and de Beauvoir's autobiography that they shared all kinds of resources, both material and otherwise. Both had numerous relationships with others, and, although this had been explicit in the case of Sartre within his lifetime, it was not generally known about de Beauvoir until after her death. Indeed, her own autobiography names as significant sexual others only Claude Lanzmann and Nelson Algren. Both men were publicly acknowledged lovers (and she in fact lived with Lanzmann for some time, in the conventional sense of actually living in the same – hers – domestic space) but the others were confined to an entirely private life. The hints at passing sexual encounters on the part of the de Beauvoir central figure in *The Mandarins* (1979a) are never replicated in her autobiography.

But after de Beauvoir's death the picture of her changed, and it changed because, inevitably, people no longer felt bound to protect the living. Yet the picture also changed because de Beauvoir had in a very real sense made it inevitable that this would happen. Her autobiography, as already suggested, had been extremely selective in its revelations. The fullest biography of her – by Deidre Bair – which had been written before her death had been considerably controlled by de Beauvoir, who had taken an active part in the construction of events and motives. The account by de Beauvoir of Sartre's final years – *La Cérémonie des adieux* – had revealed to the world the extent of Sartre's physical decline in the last 10 years of his life. This combination of control and selection about herself, and revelation about others, provided a contentious view of a private relationship which had already become both privately and publicly politicised.

The 'politicisation' of the most famous intellectual couple of the contemporary West had come about for diverse reasons. Feminism had constructed de Beauvoir as its founding mother, and then had to deal with the issue of its mother's problematic marriage. Sartre, in his final decade, had become involved with Maoist political groups whose influence de Beauvoir disliked. And finally – although by no means least – both de Beauvoir and Sartre had become involved with younger others who did not fit easily into the modus vivendi which Sartre and de Beauvoir had constructed. In both cases the relationships were with younger women (for de Beauvoir, the 'other' was a philosophy student named Sylvie le Bon de Beauvoir; for Sartre, the other was Arlette Elkaïm, also a student and also the eventual carrier of Sartre's name) and in both cases the women were officially adopted as daughters and became the legal literary executors. Between these two daughters there seems to have existed few ties of affection; their ties were with the individual parent rather than with the parental couple.

Thus in his introduction to the English edition of de Beauvoir's letters to Sartre, Quentin Hoare writes of the 'controversial maelstrom' which was unleashed around de Beauvoir within two years of her death (Hoare in de Beauvoir, 1991: vii). He points out the selectivity of de Beauvoir's account of her life and her determined manipulation of would-be biographers: 'Outsmarted, they underestimated her toughness and savvy – and turned the old iconoclast into a benign totem. How she must have chuckled into her whisky, on evenings after their earnest visits' (Hoare in de Beauvoir, 1991: viii). It is an endearing picture, with something of the clever old witch in her castle about it. Bewitched by her apparent refusal of all bourgeois behaviour and categories, numerous feminists fell victim to the apple which the older woman offered. De Beauvoir had wagered her whole life on her intelligence and her ability to compete intellectually with all-comers. This was not a woman who had ever refused to take risks or allow others to take them. In playing a determined game of concealment and revelation she was able, for much of her lifetime, to maintain a public face of integrity and autonomy. She constructed, in short, a life in which she could be a 'law unto herself'. The so clearly expressed childhood ambition was fulfilled.

Note

1. All dates given in the text for de Beauvoir's works refer to the English editions cited in the Bibliography rather than the original French editions.

2

The Woman and the Words

In the second volume of her autobiography, de Beauvoir tells us of a conversation, which turned rapidly into a quarrel, between herself and Sartre. The couple were visiting London, and over dinner Sartre, with what de Beauvoir describes as 'his usual passion for generalisation' (1962a: 144), began to outline a general theory about London's place in the universe. She writes:

> We resumed, somewhat more heatedly, the discussion that had divided us two years earlier on the heights of Saint-Cloud, and had cropped up more than once since. I maintained that reality extends beyond anything that can be said about it; that instead of reducing it to symbols capable of verbal expression, we should face it as it is – full of ambiguities, baffling and impenetrable. Sartre replied that anyone who wished, as we did, to arrange the world in a personal pattern must do something more than observe and react; he must grasp the meaning of phenomena and pin them down in words. What made nonsense of our argument was the fact that Sartre was far from understanding London after twelve days' visit, and his resumé of it omitted countless sides of his total picture: to this extent I was justified in rejecting his theory. I reacted quite differently after reading passages in his manuscript that described Le Havre: here I did get the impression that he was revealing the true essence of the place to me. But at all events this split between us was to continue for a long time: my own prime allegiance was to life, to the here-and-now reality, while for Sartre literature came

first. Still, I wanted to write and he enjoyed living, we seldom came into
open conflict. (1962a: 144)

The passage is quoted at length because it suggests much that
is important about de Beauvoir's view of the world and her relationship to knowledge. In reading philosophy, and in her own
account of her student life, she clearly found great pleasure and satisfaction in encountering explanations and understandings of the
world which were different and more convincing than her mother's
pious Catholicism and her father's cynical, right-wing nationalism.
Through philosophy, and through Sartre, she found alternative
models of the social and moral world which could allow her scope
for her own behaviour and her own values. Yet at the same time,
what the passage above gives more than a hint of, is her dissatis-
faction with the claims of philosophical systems to universal
explanation. As de Beauvoir confronted Sartre in London in the
mid-1930s, she puts forward an argument which was to reappear
later in feminism and postmodernism: namely, that the world's
diversity cannot, and indeed need not, be understood in terms of
single epistemologies. Sartre's search for a universal theory of
knowledge (the search which was to be expressed in *Being and
Nothingness* (1956) and *The Critique of Dialectical Reason* (1976))
looks, in the 1990s, like a pointless and redundant exercise,
whereas de Beauvoir's resistance has about it more than a suggestion of the way in which postmodernism was to fracture the
great universalistic expectations and assumptions of the
Enlightenment. Her plea for subjectivity and the ambiguities of
the world apparently falls on deaf ears, for Sartre is to continue, for
at least 30 years after this conversation, to 'search for a method.'

Yet among the many ironies of this discrepancy of understanding between Sartre and de Beauvoir, there lay one in
particular which was to empower de Beauvoir to construct a challenge to the absolutist epistemology to which Sartre aspired.
Through her acceptance of much the same general principles as
Sartre, de Beauvoir came to write philosophical essays – in particular *The Ethics of Ambiguity* – in which she remained true to
Sartrean principles of individualist morality (1948). But although
she began at this point, she was able to conduct a subversive discourse with Sartre's views. While Sartre was to remain convinced

that freedom was absolute, from the end of the Second World War de Beauvoir was to write both novels and essays which suggested that she was far from convinced of Sartre's ideas. The great book which was to emerge from this tension was, of course, *The Second Sex*, a consistently engaging text which radically destabilised prevalent perceptions of masculinity and femininity (1964b).

The Second Sex was published in 1949, and ever since its publication has been widely regarded as the most important book about women to have been written in the twentieth century. It was written at a time when Sartre and de Beauvoir had become jointly famous as the major inspirations of existentialism, and seen as one as far as philosophical issues were convinced. In retrospect, de Beauvoir described this period in their lives as one in which both were still a party to an individualist, and idealist, morality. Nevertheless, what de Beauvoir had explored in *The Blood of Others* (1964a), her novel about the Second World War, was the issue of constraint and obligation, and it is the tension between freedom and constraint which gives *The Second Sex* such a continuing vitality. Indeed, it is possible to read *The Second Sex* as a dialogue between de Beauvoir's own sense of the limitations of the feminine condition and her wish to accord, as firmly as possible, with Sartre's convictions about the endless possibilities of individual freedom. Throughout *The Second Sex* there is, therefore, a constant reiteration of diverse misogynist practices and ideologies and their impact on women, together with a firm assertion that the author of the book has escaped from the thrall of these perceptions by an alternative understanding of the world. The concluding message is that individual women can liberate themselves – implicitly as de Beauvoir has done – by the efforts of the mind.

Throughout *The Second Sex* de Beauvoir leaves the reader in little doubt that it is men who inflict upon women the condition and status of the 'second sex'. But to read this message simply as a description of the situation of women by an existentialist philosopher ignores the complexities of de Beauvoir's argument. In a recent collection of essays on de Beauvoir, Sonia Kruks wrote of de Beauvoir's discussion:

> Woman, then is locked in immanence by the situation man inflicts upon her – and she is not necessarily responsible for that condition. Although

the language in the passage is Sartrean, the argument is not. A consistent Sartrean position would make woman responsible for herself, no matter how constrained her situation. But for Beauvoir, women are not the primary source of the problem even though some comply with their oppressors in 'bad faith'. For many, there is no moral fault because there simply is no possibility of choice. (1992: 102)

It is this affirmation of the limits of women's situation which makes it possible to read de Beauvoir, at least in the context of *The Second Sex*, as maintaining a feminist position. As Kruks has pointed out, a 'real' Sartrean would have denied the impact of sex on the individual.

That de Beauvoir was affirming something approaching intellectual independence from Sartre is apparent from a reading of *The Second Sex*. Subsequent generations of feminists have read the book as a radical destabilisation of the categories of female and male. Judith Butler has taken this argument to its furthest limits, by arguing in *Gender Trouble* (1990: 10–12) that de Beauvoir advances the possibility in *The Second Sex* of abolishing gendered behaviour. Certainly, the book does read in some passages (particularly those on motherhood) as if de Beauvoir believes that, if only misogynist ideas could be abolished, a new, non-gendered, woman would emerge. Yet what runs throughout the book, as a kind of hidden agenda, is sexual difference, and the acceptance of masculinity and heterosexuality as *constant* constructs. Thus men remain, throughout *The Second Sex*, as implicitly desirable and masculinity, and masculine understanding as inherently superior. The 'incorrect form' of masculinity – which is misogyny – is subject to consistent critique, but at the same time there is a positive and identifiable form to masculinity which is not matched by a similar presence in femininity. For all its radical examination of the condition of women, a central core of *The Second Sex* is de Beauvoir's adherence to the idea, implicit though it is, of the connection between objectivity and universalism and masculinity. In refusing to identify with women, and being feminine in the very fundamental sense of not being a man, what de Beauvoir produces in *The Second Sex* is a book which has an ambiguous meaning for women. We can, of course, read the book as Kate Millett (1971) and Shulamith Firestone (1971) did in the early 1970s, as a straightforward attack on patriarchal gender relations, but to do so is to turn our backs on ideas about the complexities of gender relations which have been informed by over two decades of a feminism which in the West has been richly informed by psychoanalysis.

It is through the understandings and insights of psychoanalysis, as well as the experience of living in a postmodernist world, that we now read de Beauvoir. In one sense, she will always remain the great icon of twentieth century feminism, since prior to 1949 there had been few attempts to produce coherent and universalistic studies of women. But that very endeavour situates de Beauvoir as a person of her time: a time which believed in 'grand' theory and the truths of an explicit, literal, rationality. 'Reading' the world and its experiences in ways which question and problematise meaning raises a number of issues about the entirety of de Beauvoir's work.

The first, and very striking, feature of all de Beauvoir's work which it is now possible to examine is her relationship to sexuality. In her study of de Beauvoir, Jane Heath has argued cogently and persuasively that de Beauvoir's entire oeuvre is replete with the refusal of femininity. In a discussion of de Beauvoir's autobiographies, Heath (1989: 74) sets out examples of the language she uses to describe herself:

'I did not regret being a girl.'
'My education had convinced me of the intellectual inferiority of my sex.'
'Yet I did not deny any femininity.'
'I did not think of myself as "a woman" – I was me.'
'I did not deny my femininity, neither did I assume it – I did not think about it.'

The examples are particularly striking cases of negation; as Jane Heath notes, Freud made us aware that 'negation, especially when it is repeated, can be a pointer to what is repressed. In this case, it is the feminine which is repressed with considerable insistence' (1989: 74).

But the work of Freud, and the entire tradition of psychoanalysis, is not one with which de Beauvoir had great sympathy. The stumbling block, for de Beauvoir, was the theory of the unconscious, and on this she refused to shift her initial distrust and rejection of Freud's ideas. In this rejection, de Beauvoir serves as a classic example of someone who, in refusing to admit her unconscious desires, is ruled by them. De Beauvoir's ambiguity about femininity (even if it is described only thus and not in the stronger terms of fear and suspicion) runs as a current throughout her work, and is an ambiguity which she consistently attempts to resolve through either the literal or metaphorical presence of the phallus. To elaborate: in her first published novel, *She Came to Stay*, de Beauvoir's central female character, Françoise, kills off the woman, Xavière, who threatens the relationship of Françoise and her lover Pierre (1966). So far, so ordinary, since we can read this as a fictional representation of conventional heterosexual jealousy. Yet what is also very much part of this novel is Françoise's own love for Xavière, a homosexual love which is as disturbing to Françoise as any of Xavière's antics. The Pierre/Xavière relationship is, after all, only one more incident in Pierre's history of sexual promiscuity. The truly disturbing eroticism in the novel is not, therefore, Pierre's philandering, but Françoise's sense of unease and disquiet when confronted by her own desire for a woman. For a woman like Françoise, who prides herself on her 'masculine' independence and autonomy, the spectre of the feminine is deeply disturbing. Françoise, as much as being the name of the central character in *She Came to Stay* is also the name of de Beauvoir's mother, and it is difficult to see the naming of this character as an entirely accidental coincidence, since within the one person is located a range of possibility. Françoise seems to have quasi-maternal feelings towards Xavière, as well as the glimmering of sexual attraction towards her, but it is finally heterosexuality, in the explicit, blatant, destruction of the feminine and sexual relationships between women, which triumphs. The novel's initial French title, *Légitime Défense*, is one of those many transparent phrases in de Beauvoir: here, the 'legitimate' defence against the literal and metaphorical invasion of autonomy of women by women is made explicit.

'Women: Keep Out and Keep Off' could be an appropriate sign for the novels which follow *She Came to Stay*. Both *The Blood of Others* (1964a) and to a lesser extent *All Men are Mortal* (1955) marginalise women and present women as a constraint on masculinity and on masculine action. *The Blood of Others* has a male narrator and chronicles the feelings of a Resistance fighter, Jean Blomart, as he watches his lover, Hélène, die. Blomart cannot escape the feeling that he is in some way responsible for Hélène's death and the novel is, in a sense, an attempt to make Blomart feel better about his actions. What we have to ask is why de Beauvoir needed to help Blomart assuage his guilt; perhaps feelings of guilt and responsibility were appropriate in the circumstances. As it is, Hélène dies having made sure that her last words are a further exoneration of her beloved. Undeveloped, although present, in the novel are hints at the different costs to women and men of war. The terrible suffering of women who lose their children is a recurrent theme throughout *The Blood of Others*, yet this issue – with its obvious implications for the question of the different relationship of women and men to war – is consistently refused and allowed only in descriptive terms.

But it is in de Beauvoir's lengthiest and more developed novel, *The Mandarins* (1979a), that we find her more explicit discussion of sexuality and heterosexuality. The novel, like much of de Beauvoir's fiction, draws heavily on events of her own life, and in particular her affair with the American writer Nelson Algren. In this affair, in which de Beauvoir was to admit that she experienced a sexual happiness and fulfilment hitherto unknown, a new form of sexuality and sexual relations appeared – one which was not primarily mediated and lived through shared intellectual projects. De Beauvoir, in her autobiographical account of Algren, does not assign to him the intellectual power of Sartre. On the other hand, what Algren does do is react to de Beauvoir as a sexual other and a sexual partner. In her autobiography de Beauvoir describes how her affair with Algren begins through her wish to be with 'a man of her own' (1965a: 126). In *The Mandarins*, the feeling is described as the wish 'to live, really live', in New York: 'I have to walk in the streets holding the arm of a man who provisionally at least, would be mine' (1979a: 403).

Thus Algren (the Brogan character in *The Mandarins*) comes to be 'the man' of the author of *The Second Sex*. The affair is intense, sexually passionate and ends unhappily. *The Mandarins* is dedicated to Algren, and the Brogan embodiment of himself is a sympathetic character, but for the real-life Algren the book represented a massive betrayal of trust on the part of Simone de Beauvoir. He was to remark in an interview some time after the novel's publication that 'even in the whore-houses they close the doors' and to describe de Beauvoir in terms which were less than flattering (Algren, 1965: 135). The invasion of privacy which *The Mandarins* constituted to Algren was apparently not a problem to de Beauvoir: for her, *roman à clef* was an acceptable form of the novel and a worthy tribute to Algren and their relationship.

Since it is now possible to review the completed works of de Beauvoir, we can read *The Mandarins* in a number of ways: as a straightforward exercise in narrative realism which chronicles the lives of the post-war French intelligentsia; as a hymn of praise to Nelson Algren; or as an assertion of independence by a woman who is gradually becoming more sure of herself and more pre-pared to identify with women and assert her own values. All readings are possible, but it is the last which might enable us to explore the pattern of de Beauvoir's work, and her complex rela-tionship within it to the feminine and femininity. As we have seen, up to a certain extent (and including *The Mandarins*), de Beauvoir remains absolutely true to heterosexuality as the ideal form of interpersonal relationships. This is not to say that all heterosexual relationships *are* ideal, or that they are necessarily perfectly realised and without pain and conflict. De Beauvoir is enough of a realist to allow that these possibilities exist. But what she does do is to picture the fullest form of emotional commitment as situated entirely within heterosexuality; all the major relationships of her fiction up to and including 1954 are premised on the idea that heterosexuality is the ideal form of human relationship. In doing this, de Beauvoir is, of course, only doing what a major tradition in Western culture asserts; the cultural 'fit' between her work and the dominant culture is therefore very close. We can observe that a consistent subtext to this theme is that of the dependant woman – Paula of *The Mandarins*, Suzanne of *She Came to Stay* and the nar-rator of *A Woman Destroyed* – but these women only serve to demonstrate de Beauvoir's argument, that while valorising hetero-sexuality, women must not become dependent on individual men. As the central character of *She Came to Stay* says of Suzanne: 'Suzanne belonged to the tribe of victims. She accepted anything from Claude – but we belong to a different species, we are strong and free and live our own lives' (1966: 74).

Being 'strong' and 'free' means, in the context of de Beauvoir's novels, being financially independent, generally childless and involved in 'meaningful' (that is liberal/professional) paid work. All these attributes are absolutely the stuff of which traditional liberal, feminist demands in Western cultures are made, yet what is striking about de Beauvoir's early work, and indeed early life, is that there is no mention in it of *any* inspiration or motivation that suggests a relationship to organised feminism. The inspirational source about how to live is clearly that of conventional masculinity: the 'strong' women characters of these novels apparently have interesting jobs, education and income through fortuitous circumstances. What is missing in all these accounts of female strength and independence is how the women got like that.

Thus accounting for the appearance of female strength in de Beauvoir's early fiction takes us back to de Beauvoir and her experience of the getting of both education and professional qualifications. In the third volume of her autobiography, *Force of Circumstance*, de Beauvoir raises the issue of how she came to write *The Second Sex* and her own experiences of becoming a woman. What she does is to offer an explanation about herself and relationship to her own femininity which begins with Sartre and then returns to her childhood. Thus:

> The man whom I placed above all others did not consider me inferior to men. I had many male friends whose eyes, far from imprisoning me within set limits, recognised me as a human being in my own right. Such good fortune had protected me against all resentment and all bitterness; my readers will know too that I was never infected by such feelings during my childhood or my adolescence. Subtler readers concluded that I was a misogynist and that, while pretending to take up the cudgels for women, I was damning them; this is untrue. I do not praise them to the skies and I have anatomised all these defects engendered by their condition, but I also showed their good qualities and their merits. (1965a: 189)

In the same passage de Beauvoir speaks of how fortunate she feels to have been able to enjoy the privileges of both sexes; she regarded herself as fortunate in having achieved success as a writer to such an extent that at parties 'the wives all got together and talked to each other while I talked to the men, who nevertheless behaved toward me with greater courtesy than they did toward the members of their own sex' (1965a: 189).

This would be a fairly breathtaking remark for a feminist in the 1990s; to write as a woman about women as 'they', to deny flatly any feelings of resentment at female subordination, and to accord the conversation of men a greater importance than the conversation of women, all smack of what has come to be known as the 'Queen Bee' syndrome. Since *Memoirs of a Dutiful Daughter* includes much material about the very conventional attitudes of de Beauvoir's parents towards the education of girls and its value, the passage also reads as simply untrue. It is interesting that in writing as she did in *Force of Circumstance*, de Beauvoir herself may have felt that she had misrepresented her case, since she includes a footnote which points out that resentment and bitterness are some-times perfectly justifiable. No doubt many readers would agree with that sentiment; they might also go a step further and suggest that what de Beauvoir has written in this account of the writing of *The Second Sex* is an exercise in distancing herself in fairly unam-biguous terms from both the conditions which inspire feminism (that is a massive sense of injustice at the gender inequalities of the world) and from feminism itself. It is not so much that feminism existed as a coherent ideology at the time of writing of either *The Second Sex* or *Force of Circumstance*, but it clearly existed for de Beauvoir as an unspoken possibility. Thus even without an exter-nal, organised movement named feminism (which was to emerge as an undeniable and public force in the late 1960s and early 1970s), what de Beauvoir clearly recognised, albeit in a subliminal way, was the possibility of a generalised set of experiences which could give rise to questions about her own relationship with both masculinity and femininity. Denying these possibilities was essen-tial for a woman whose very identity had been constructed through identification with masculinity; nevertheless, given the extremely programmatic conclusion to *The Second Sex*, it is surprising that de Beauvoir did not feel inclined to become part of an organised movement related to the condition of women.

But what de Beauvoir did do after completing *The Second Sex* was to return to fiction and to autobiography. *Memoirs of a Dutiful Daughter* was published in 1958, *The Prime of Life* in 1960, *Force of Circumstance* in 1963 and *All Said and Done* in 1972. She also com-pleted a short account of the death of her mother, which appeared in 1964 (1965b). The various volumes of the autobiography, particularly *Memoirs*, were extremely successful and of course marked the beginning of the de Beauvoir industry. Once *Memoirs* was published, Simone de Beauvoir's life, quite as much as her work, became a subject of comment and discussion. Thus it is impossible not to mention, at this point, the contrast between de Beauvoir and Sartre on the issue of autobiography: de Beauvoir wrote four volumes of conventional autobiography and two others which concern specific events in her life *(A Very Easy Death* and *Adieux: Farewell to Sartre)*. This adds up to a great many words. In contrast, Sartre was abstemious in the extreme in his discussion of his life: *Words* (1964b) was his single contribution and it is an extremely slim volume.

This contrast might once have been put down to individual difference, but to a generation educated in psychoanalysis and an awareness of gender differences in writing and relationship to words, the minimalism of Sartre versus the extravagance of de Beauvoir is an irresistible cause for comment. It was not, after all, that in other contexts Sartre was an economical writer; on the contrary, many of his best known philosophical works are of expansive length, as are his biographical studies of Jean Genet (1963) and Flaubert (1981). But, apart from length, what is most significant about de Beauvoir and Sartre's respective autobiographies is the presence and absence of the other. Sartre to a large extent dominates de Beauvoir's autobiography; *Memoirs* can be read as a search for a new hero after the disappointment with father-as-hero. Fortunately for de Beauvoir that hero appears, in the shape of Sartre, and from then on he is the central character who organises much of the emotional and intellectual state of de Beauvoir. If Sartre is happy and fulfilled, so on the whole is de Beauvoir. The only times when his happiness and fulfilment do not chord with hers are those when Sartre is clearly preoccupied with another woman. Since by his own admission Sartre experiences the world through women (on his various travels he frequently either had affairs with, or proposed to, interpreters who were women), de Beauvoir had to come to terms with his lavish enjoyment of women. Since the pattern was rapidly made apparent, de Beauvoir seems to have been largely untroubled by it, although the affairs with Olga, Dolores Vanetti and Arlette Elkaïm clearly disturbed the equilibrium of the relationship between Sartre and de Beauvoir. We do not have information from Sartre about his feelings for de Beauvoir, and her relationships with other men. That side of the story is simply not there. We can therefore conjecture that either for Sartre the relationship did not merit extensive documentation, or he did not wish to write about his 'private' life, or he chose other subjects. At all events, the couple followed the age old maxim which suggests that for men love is peripheral, while for women it is their very existence.

Thus there is about de Beauvoir's autobiography a quality which is supremely feminine: despite the long passages (which are significantly longer in *Force of Circumstance* and *All Said and Done* than in the previous two volumes) which describe political events, the essential dynamic of the autobiography is the author's relationships with other people, and one man in particular. Sartre is quoted endlessly, Sartre explains events to de Beauvoir and, not infrequently, Sartre upsets and disturbs de Beauvoir by his relationships with other women. There is, throughout the auto-biography, no hint of another side to this partnership: a situation in which de Beauvoir upset and disturbed Sartre. Women, the unwritten agenda goes, do not matter in the same way as men.

The 'femininity' of de Beauvoir's autobiography lies, therefore, in its subject matter and its organising theme. The tragedy of the last years of the relationship between Sartre and de Beauvoir was that it was marked by jealousies and rivalries between de Beauvoir and the younger people (both female and male) with whom Sartre surrounded himself. Arlette Elkaïm (subsequently adopted by Sartre as his daughter) was one cause of difficulty, and Benny Lévy, a Maoist who became Sartre's secretary, was another. Again, there is an asymmetrical situation: de Beauvoir disliked and distrusted both Lévy and Elkaïm, Sartre seemed entirely uncon-cerned about de Beauvoir's relationship with Sylvie le Bon and her own eventual adoption of Sylvie. Yet if these individuals provided the context of the tragedy (and the source of many of the contests after Sartre's death for control of both his estate and the public construction of his history), the nature of the tragedy for de Beauvoir was her identification with the masculine world of knowl-edge and public 'words'. She had made the relationship with Sartre into one which was formal and cerebral; the distancing use of 'vous' in their conversations suggested an avoidance and refusal of intimacy which separated their relationship from relationships with others. De Beauvoir, throughout Sartre's life, had acted as his first reader, in many ways (and instances) his conscience and his superego. For Sartre, who had been brought up by his mother, and lost his father at an early age, de Beauvoir was to take over many of the functions of the male parent, the adult person who 'judged' the child.

What this structure did was to give the relationship both the potential for considerable longevity and the potential for ultimate collapse. Even if the relationship never actually collapsed (in large part because Sartre died first), what happened in the last years of his life was clearly transforming it. De Beauvoir from the early 1970s had moved closer to women (the friendship with Sylvie le Bon dated from an earlier period, the beginning of the 1960s) in both a personal and a theoretical sense. Men, and the masculine, no longer appeared to have the same attraction for her, and she was to say in an interview that for her women 'are more desirable than men'; this was because, she suggested:

> [women] are more attractive, softer, their skin is nicer. And generally they have more charm. It is quite often the case with the usual married couple that the woman is nicer, more lively, more attractive, more amusing, even on an intellectual level. (Schwarzer, 1984: 108–9)

These remarks, which might be nothing out of the ordinary for many feminists, were made by the same woman who had written of her delight at being able to talk to 'the men' at social gatherings while the women remained locked in their own conversation. Although de Beauvoir was to refuse and reject the idea that there was such a thing as an essential female nature, it is apparent that at least by the beginning of the 1970s her sense of gender identity was beginning to shift. The woman who had succeeded in a male world was now beginning to question, not just the intellectual products of that world, but the very processes through which they were constructed. This shift in perception is most apparent through the relationship with Sartre: throughout her life he remained a kind of metaphorical, generalised phallus: patriarchal knowledge embodied in a human form.

Inevitably, therefore, the distant, formal form of address of 'vous' was appropriate for this relationship. De Beauvoir was not just addressing a human being, she was addressing a system of knowledge when she spoke to Sartre, and a system of knowledge which had manifestly informed and structured much of her work. For many years, certainly throughout the unproductive 1930s, and then in the much more productive 1940s, de Beauvoir's relationship to Sartre and *his* words could remain unproblematic. In the 1930s she had not found her voice; indeed, it was the threat of the loss of Sartre to Olga and the discovery of her own deeply ambivalent feelings about Olga which allowed her voice to emerge. During the 1940s and to a large extent the 1950s de Beauvoir and Sartre had a public identity as a couple because of their politics and because de Beauvoir's affair with Algren gave her relationship with Sartre a greater degree of equality. She had 'her' North American, just as he had his in Dolores Vanetti. Thus history, both general and individual, helped to maintain a relationship.

In the 1960s and 1970s, as a new form of politics emerged in Western Europe, it is apparent from a number of sources (biographies of both Sartre and de Beauvoir, comments by both parties and numerous others) that the effects of these politics on the two individuals was seismatic.[1] Politics after 1968 throughout Europe began to shift from a set of formal allegiances to monolithic political parties to a more disparate politics of coalitions of interest. It is, of course, the case that the Western European *state* is still organised around the idea of competing political parties, but the old exclusive identification of politics with formal political parties disappeared. Feminism began to create women's organisations, the consciousness of race and ethnic differences gave rise to the politics of racial difference, and across both gender and racial lines groups of people organised around issues related to the arms race, the environment and the relationship of the North to the South. Politics became, in short, diverse and plural and the politics with which both Sartre and de Beauvoir were familiar started to disappear.

So as history changed the face of European politics, it also changed the nature of the relationship between Sartre and de Beauvoir. Both were essentially products of 'modern' Europe, they had named the journal *Les Temps Modernes* after Chaplin's film and identified with the possibilities of a technologically sophisticated world. But they were not 'post-modern', in that both had spent the greater part of their intellectual maturity seeking (in Sartre's case explicitly) for a universal epistemology. De Beauvoir 'modernised', in the face of these shifts in European intellectual history, more rapidly than Sartre. Although in the last 20 years of her life she still explicitly maintained many of the ideas of her youth, she nevertheless began to move towards a more pluralistic understanding of the social world. In her last great novel, *The Woman Destroyed*, she abandoned the narrative realism of her previous fiction and produced a sparse and vivid account of subjectivity which is entirely different from the quasi-objectivity of her earlier novels (1979b). She consistently refused to accept the 'new' French feminism of Irigaray, Cixous and Wittig and was particularly vehement on the subject of language. For her language remained 'fixed' and neutral; even if she was prepared to entertain the hardly radical idea that women and men use language differently, she was not prepared to accept the far more disturbing ideas which Irigaray in particular advanced, that for women and men language is not just used differently, but actually *is* different.

While de Beauvoir was exploring feminism in the 1970s and 1980s, Sartre became involved with Maoism: again, the difference is marked, if not surprising. In interviews with de Beauvoir towards the end of his life, Sartre appeared all too ready to admit his misogyny and his patriarchal attitudes, but he was clearly disinclined to make connections between these attitudes to women and his thinking about the world in general. It was this compartmentalisation which remained to the end; thinking about women could be 'improved', in the sense of being made more politically correct, but this did not necessarily make any difference to anything else. Making connections between thinking about sexuality, about herself as a woman *and* the organisation of the world, was clearly a point which de Beauvoir was getting close to by the time of her death. Her intellectual shift, which dates from the mid-1960s, saw a change in both the organisation of her daily life and her intellectual and political priorities. In summary, women became the *explicit* central concern of her life.

Note

1. See the comments by Deidre Bair (1990) in the case of de Beauvoir and Cohen-Solal (1987) for Sartre.

3

The Woman and
Women

The previous chapter dealt, briefly, with de Beauvoir's great work on women, *The Second Sex*. The comments made in that chapter may suggest to readers a critical reading of *The Second Sex*, and that inference would be entirely correct. But like many readings of *The Second Sex*, however critical, it is nevertheless a reading which begins at the point of accepting the importance of the book, and its manifest contribution to the intellectual history of the twentieth century. The book was first published (in two volumes) in 1949, although extracts from it had been serialised in *Les Temps Modernes* prior to its publication in book form.[1]

These bald facts about publication clearly reveal little about the origin of *The Second Sex* or its eventual impact on European thought. In her memoirs de Beauvoir credits Sartre with the suggestion that she should write about women and in those memoirs there is no hint that de Beauvoir saw anything the slightest bit ironical in this suggestion, or felt any need to raise even one eyebrow at Sartre's motivation in making it. Since 'other women' had figured so large in the de Beauvoir/Sartre relationship (and since at the time Sartre was involved in an extraordinarily disruptive relationship with the woman named as 'M'), the suggestion now looks very much as if Sartre was handing to de Beauvoir the intellectual task of enabling him to understand women, and the pattern of his relations with them.

Once given her homework, de Beauvoir set off with great enthusiasm to find out about this extraordinary tribe called women. Her method in constructing *The Second Sex* was clearly to follow all entries in the library catalogue on women and then organise these entries within a theoretical framework of existentialism. As anyone with even a passing interest in feminism knows, what emerged was a very fully illustrated thesis about woman as 'the other' in Western civilisation. The concept of 'the other' had long been an organising principle of the existentialist philosophy of Sartre and de Beauvoir, but the shift which occurs in *The Second Sex* is towards understanding 'the other' in social as well as individual terms. Thus in effect what de Beauvoir was to do in *The Second Sex* was to generalise 'the other': to move away from the already radical construction of 'the other' which was part of her early fiction, and towards an even more innovative theory about the relative freedom of individuals within a social context.

Until recently, the conventional wisdom about the theoretical origins of *The Second Sex* was that they lay in the existentialist philosophy forged by Sartre and de Beauvoir (but particularly Sartre) in the early 1940s. This reading of theoretical underpinning is one which assigns (as is conventionally the case) the man-in-the-case with the credit for naming and working out the problem, while the woman occupies the position (as is expected) of the intellectual subordinate who provides information and material. This portrayal of the Sartre/de Beauvoir intellectual partnership is one which makes Sartre the project director and de Beauvoir the research assistant. Even if – as in this case – the research assistant goes off with one of the master's best ideas and writes one of the great books of the twentieth century, the relationship is nevertheless seen in terms of the traditional expectation of male intellectual creativity and female intellectual passivity.

This traditional expectation has now been widely questioned, for the two very good reasons that quite a lot of 'male' ideas are inadequate and because we now know that there have been numerous 'female' ideas which have received inadequate attention. A new reading of intellectual history assesses more critically the given judgements of intellectual history. Given this, the relative contributions of Sartre and de Beauvoir to existentialism and to each other's work are now being rewritten with a much greater emphasis on de Beauvoir as an innovative and creative thinker. Feminism, in fact, is doing what de Beauvoir refused to do: passing a critical eye over the claims to originality of Sartre and de Beauvoir (see, for example, Moi, 1994). De Beauvoir played the part of the supportive wife to Sartre throughout her life: time and again she voiced the view that he was the creative thinker, while her role was to develop and illustrate his ideas.[2] For many years this account of the intellectual partnership was accepted as the actual version of reality; the famous biographical note on de Beauvoir (reprinted in all Penguin editions of her work) that in her final examinations 'she was placed second to Sartre' was allowed to stand as an assessment of their relative philosophical worth and standing.

De Beauvoir's own refusal of her intellectual competence is part of a pattern in her life in which she identified intellectually and sexually with her father and emotionally with her mother. Throughout the 50 years of her relationship with Sartre, she behaved in all respects in the relationship as her father had done in his marriage: thoroughly promiscuous and fully involved, in all senses, in public affairs. Yet at the same time as she did this, she also adopted the stubborn fidelity to the relationship which her mother had shown to her marriage. As Françoise de Beauvoir had persistently refused to challenge her husband's authority, so de Beauvoir consistently allowed Sartre the dominant and the creative intellectual role.

Yet what de Beauvoir could consciously and explicitly deny, she could not prevent from emerging in her work. Thus in contemporary reassessments of her work (and its relationship to that of Sartre), a much greater emphasis is being placed on de Beauvoir's contribution and the ways in which it emerged. Central to this overall rereading, and to an understanding of *The Second Sex*, is de Beauvoir's first novel, *She Came to Stay*. A perfectly credible reading of *She Came to Stay* is that it is concerned with the retelling of the time in de Beauvoir's own life when a woman named Olga threatened her relationship with Sartre. The narrative strength of the novel owes much to the telling of this commonplace tale of jealousy and revenge. Indeed, there is no reason to abandon this reading of *She Came to Stay*. However, what it is important to do, in the context of a discussion of the relative contributions of Sartre and de Beauvoir to philosophy and the theoretical underpinnings of *The Second Sex*, is to examine *She Came to Stay* less as a novel and more as a treatise in philosophy. If we shift that emphasis then what emerges is a theoretical text about appearance and reality and the nature of the other.

Any reader of *She Came to Stay* will be struck by the discursiveness of the novel, and the way in which de Beauvoir frequently presents to the reader examples of the same action or phenomenon. As Kate Fullbrook and Edward Fullbrook (1993) have recently pointed out, this is particularly true in the case of discussion of the body; indeed, the age-old mind/body problem is one of the central themes of the novel. As the Fullbrooks explain:

> These passages [in *She Came to Stay*] exhibit and contrast four ways of experiencing the human body, distinctions which were later partially echoed in Ryle's *Concept of Mind* (1949), and which provided a highly original way around the classic mind/body problem in Sartre's *Being and Nothingness*. The fourfold distinction is as follows: there is my body as part of my lived subjectivity, that is, the instrument by which I am in-the-world; there is my body as seen by others; there are the bodies of others; and there are bodies construed as purely physical objects (the 'body' of Cartesian dualism). Beauvoir's nightclub scene self-consciously shifts back and forth between these four philosophical points of view. The third-person narrator presents the bodies of others: the young woman staring and speaking to her companion, the woman with feathers looking at a man's hand, Xavière doing things to her arm, the feathered woman conversing, and Xavière touching and talking to herself. But Françoise's consciousness is also presented, and hence her unselfconscious experiencing of her body as her means of thinking, hearing and speaking. These two modes of experiencing the human body (as an object belonging to another subjectivity and as part of one's own subjectivity) are found in most narratives; it is Beauvoir's structured weaving of the other two modes through the scene that shows her philosophical intent. The two women coping with male flirtations are contrasted by the way they respond to the possibility of experiencing their bodies as objects of another's subjectivity. The woman with the emblematic feathers in her hair decides to experience her arm as a mere thing impersonally related to her consciousness. Similarly, the reader's attention is drawn to 'the fine down' on Xavière's skin. Beauvoir's description of touching one's own eyelashes illustrates the unbridgeable difference

between experiencing one's body as the instrument of one's subjectivity and experiencing it as an object. In *Being and Nothingness*, Sartre also uses the example of touching oneself to introduce his discussion of the body and its modes of being. (1993: 99–100)

The point which they are making is essentially that although *She Came to Stay* is a novel in the orthodox, narrative, sense, it is also a philosophical treatise, and a treatise which prefigures in a number of important ways the systematic philosophical ideas set out by Sartre in *Being and Nothingness*. As the Fullbrooks tellingly state, both *She Came to Stay* and *Being and Nothingness* were published in 1943 but *She Came to Stay* had been drafted, and read by Sartre some time before he began work and then during working, on his manuscript. Far from de Beauvoir's novel illustrating Sartre's ideas, there would appear to be a very considerable case for supposing that Sartre's thesis was made possible by de Beauvoir's novel.

Nevertheless, whatever the precise source of Sartre or de Beauvoir's ideas, the ownership and origin of intellectual ideas has always to be regarded critically. We cannot know for certain how either party derived their ideas, or even if only two people were engaged in their development. What is important is that in *She Came to Stay* de Beauvoir wrote a novel in which she addressed two of the most long-standing issues of Western philosophy, namely the gap between appearance and reality, and the implications for knowledge of the existence of the other. This latter issue, that of the question of the existence of other people as conscious beings, has long preoccupied philosophers; it was to be the central theme of *She Came to Stay*, and the organising theme of *The Second Sex*. In short, the issue is that of how 'the other' and 'the others' are constructed by an individual, and how other people have not only an understanding and interest in themselves, but equally in other people. As Françoise says at the beginning of *She Came to Stay*:

'It's almost impossible to believe that other people are conscious beings, aware of their own inward feelings, as we ourselves are aware of our own', said Françoise. 'To me it's terrifying when we grasp that. We get the impression of no longer being anything but a figment of someone else's mind.' (1966: 12)

In that final sentence lies, of course the origin of *The Second Sex* – the idea that women have had little or no control over the

construction of their own objectivity (or indeed subjectivity) but
have been constructed through the understanding, or misunder-
standing, of men.

In documenting misogyny, as de Beauvoir was to do in *The
Second Sex*, she taps one of the two great prejudices of the West –
the other being anti-Semitism. The theme of *The Second Sex*, which
de Beauvoir resolutely addresses in the introduction, is the question of *why* men should have won domination over women. As she
asks, 'How is it that this world has always belonged to the men and
that things have begun to change only recently?' (1964b: xxi). De
Beauvoir follows this question by asking what can change, and
whether or not change would be positive. In the light of what follows, few readers could answer in anything except the affirmative,
since what de Beauvoir presents is a rich catalogue of misogyny,
prejudice and discrimination. In this examination she is on
extremely thick ice, in that any reading of what passed until
recently as 'Western civilisation' was largely Western male civilisation. Feminism in the 1970s and 1980s largely accepted the idea
that from the reputed dawn of our civilisation women played little
or no part in the construction of public life. Only as people began
to exert control over nature was it possible for a minority of women
to begin to claim a voice in the making of the public world.

This emphasis on the public is deliberate, since much of *The
Second Sex* is about women's limited participation in the public
sphere. But one of the very radical strengths of the book is that de
Beauvoir is as much concerned with what is described as 'the private' as the public. Unlike many early feminists, whose concerns
(for good reason) were about the limited participation of women in
the public world, de Beauvoir opens up the discussion to include a
systematic discussion of personal relationships between the sexes.
She enters the private space, and with a determined and critical eye
examines the patterns of emotional collusion between women and
men which make possible the status of the woman as inferior and
the man as superior. The introduction of *The Second Sex* is written
with passion, and with passionate contempt for men who have an
innate conviction of their own superiority. As a high achieving intellectual, de Beauvoir writes scathingly of those men whose own
intellectual competence is so inadequate that they have to

infantilise women in order to maintain their sense of superiority.
She writes:

> But men profit in many more subtle ways from the otherness, the alter-
> ity of woman. Here is miraculous balm for those afflicted with an
> inferiority complex, and indeed no one is more arrogant toward women
> than the man who is anxious about his virility. (1964b: xxv)

Defined and condemned in two sentences, the all too familiar
Western male emerges: emotionally inadequate, fearful, endlessly
locked into competition with other men and with no resources
except the very important one of dominating women. This male
person is the archetypical fascist of *The Authoritarian Personality*
and the authoritarian fearful of femininity and affectivity (Adorno et
al., 1969). Indeed, it is interesting that both de Beauvoir and members of the Frankfurt School turned to a critical examination of
conventional masculinity at exactly the same historical moment of
Western awareness of the Holocaust and its implications. Even
though de Beauvoir, perhaps remembering the men she knew, is
careful to qualify her remarks by conceding that not all men
actively seek the domination of women, she has established a ten-
dency, an impulse, in masculinity which is to run through *The
Second Sex*.

De Beauvoir is not, however, an impatient writer, and so she is
careful not to address initially the question of what is to be done
about this situation. Her first, and considerable, interest is in the
discussion of the origin of woman's 'otherness'. Her agenda, therefore, is less that of programmatic feminism and more that of
explanation and understanding. What she does with her agenda is
to present systematically collected evidence to demonstrate the
extent to which women have been refused access to the category
of human being – a category which de Beauvoir sees men as having fully occupied. Women, on the other hand, are not *human*, in
the same sense of having transcended their biology and having
become both more than their biological gender and fully in control
of their place in the social and ideological world. In the 1990s it is
difficult to read this idea of men as transcendent with anything
less than scepticism; contemporary feminism and the very project
of postmodernity have so undermined rigid gender constructions
that the identification of men and humanity is highly questionable.

But de Beauvoir is not writing in the 1990s, and, although she has highly developed modern inclinations, she is hardly a post-modern. Nevertheless, what she does in *The Second Sex* is to make a major contribution to our contemporary understanding of gender, in that she radically disturbs sexual identity and the concept of a 'fixed' sexual identity. In this, of course, she follows Freud and even though she has little sympathy with psychoanalysis (the concept of the unconscious is too much for a rationalist like de Beauvoir to accept) she nevertheless shares with Freud the crucially important idea that there is no such thing as a 'natural' woman or man. De Beauvoir's major stated difference with Freud is that she reads him as a determinist, whereas she wishes 'to place woman in a world of values and give her behaviour a dimension of liberty'. She makes, in passing, the telling remark that psychoanalysis substitutes normality for morality, and goes on to argue that acting 'as a woman is also a delusion: to be a woman would mean to be the object, the *other* – and the other nevertheless remains subject in the midst of her resignation' (1964b: 45).

Thus what de Beauvoir is doing here, and throughout *The Second Sex*, is dealing essentially with the language and the words which construct the idea, the condition of 'woman'. Although she includes an extensive discussion of the physical condition of women's lives (their biology and sexuality and the experience of motherhood in particular), she is more concerned with the ideological construction of these specific experiences than with their impact on women and women's own understanding. As numerous critics have pointed out, de Beauvoir's account of women's sexuality, of motherhood and of social life is overwhelmingly structured by a perception of something relatively better – the relatively better in this case being the nature of men's experiences. Obviously, *The Second Sex* was written at a time (and in a country) in which women's access to contraception was limited if not non-existent and in which their sexual lives were dominated by discourses of male sexual needs and female sexual passivity; but even allowing that de Beauvoir is writing about France in the 1940s (a country which banned contraception and guillotined abortionists), she is using this historical evidence to demonstrate a general, transhistorical point.

Reading *The Second Sex* in the context of contemporary feminism (and feminist psychoanalysis), it is difficult not to read it as a cry of resistance against the symbolic order by a woman who feels excluded from it by virtue of her sex. Thus a considerable section of the book deals with myths and fiction explicitly, while a great deal of the rest of the book uses literature as evidence about social attitudes. This method was replicated by (among others) Kate Millett in *Sexual Politics* (1971) and, as various critics have pointed out, raises problems not only about the selection of the texts chosen, but also the way in which they are read. To read Montherlant, D.H. Lawrence, Claudel, Breton and Stendhal as de Beauvoir does in *The Second Sex* is to produce a catalogue of misogynist remarks and hostilities towards women. Given the nature of the work of these men, it is inevitable that an 'anti-women' reading should result. Yet alongside that expressed antagonism there also lies a fear and an envy of women, not least because women, in their very lack of apparent social and historical freedom, are also removed from the problems, the antagonisms and the hatred of that public 'free' world. It is not that the private world of women is free of problems (or in any sense a world of liberty), but it *is* a place in which women can construct independent and rewarding ties with others.

This issue, of the form of ties-to-others, dominates *The Second Sex*, and with it the legacy of de Beauvoir to feminism. The conclusion of *The Second Sex* assumes, in the same way as Engels, that the economic liberation of women (by which both mean the end of women's economic dependence on individual men rather than liberation from any particular economic system) will liberate women (Engels, 1985). At the same time, de Beauvoir exhorts women to live 'independent' lives, as independent, as Margaret Walters has pointed out, as the most Protestant hero could possibly be (1976). The chapters in which de Beauvoir considers the various possible conditions of women's lives (Childhood, The Young Girl, The Lesbian, The Married Woman, The Mother) are all essentially records of the difficulty, and the threat to personal autonomy, of these relationships. In childhood and adolescence, de Beauvoir argues, women are robbed of responsibility for their own future:

> the adolescent girl does not think herself responsible for her future; she sees no use in demanding much of herself since her lot in the end will not depend on her own efforts. Far from consigning herself to man

because she recognises her inferiority, it is because she is thus con-
signed to him that, accepting the idea of her inferiority, she establishes
its truth. (1964b: 313)

Once married (and married, de Beauvoir assumes, within a middle
class discourse of marriage-as-a-career), women attempt to construct a life through the home and the husband:

In the early years of marriage the wife often fills herself with illusions,
she tries to admire her husband whole heartedly to love him unreservedly, to feel herself indispensable to him and the children. And
then her true sentiments become clear; she sees that her husband
could get along very well without her, that her children are bound to get
away from her and to be always more or less ungrateful. The home no
longer saves her from empty liberty; she finds herself alone, forlorn, a
subject; and she finds nothing to do with herself. (1964b: 450)

In this passage de Beauvoir writes of two biographical experiences: her own and that of her mother. In *The Prime of Life* she had
told readers how, after the establishment of her relationship with
Sartre, she was content to stagnate (as she retrospectively presented it) in happiness. She describes how Sartre had turned to
her in these early days and expressed the hope that she would not
become 'a female introvert'. The expression 'female introvert' is
that of Sartre, but, as I noted earlier, what de Beauvoir does with it
is to translate it into 'housewife'. She writes:

There was, indeed, no danger of my turning into a mere housewife, but
he compared me to those heroines of Meredith's who after a long battle
for their independence ended up quite content to be some man's help-
meet. I was furious with myself for disappointing him in this way.
(1962a: 61)

How exactly like a conventional woman, contemporary feminist
readers might note, for women to take responsibility for the emo-
tions of men. If Sartre was 'disappointed', this reading would
continue, then he should have revised his understanding of the
human condition in order to include the experiences and expectations of women.

But de Beauvoir was not listening to Sartre's 'disappointment' in
the 1990s, or writing *The Second Sex* in such a context. She was
writing *The Prime of Life* and *The Second Sex* as testaments to a generation of women who had had to fight hard to be allowed the most

minimal social and educational freedoms. The battles for the now taken-for-granted liberties of movement and thought were inevitably part of de Beauvoir's history, a general history sharpened by the observation of her mother's life. The passage quoted above in which she describes the rapid transformation of the joys of early marriage into petty disappointments is exactly like those passages in *Memoirs of a Dutiful Daughter* in which she described the shift in her parents' marriage from joyful intimacy to conflict and disappointment. The children whom de Beauvoir describes as 'more or less ungrateful' might well be de Beauvoir and her sister. As *Memoirs* makes clear, de Beauvoir's mother became a rigorous observer of her daughter's behaviour and much of the attention was unwelcome. Françoise de Beauvoir and her fate informs much of the discussion of marriage and motherhood in *The Second Sex*, but precisely because of this auto/biographical source the writing on these issues has a passion and a fury about it which has seldom been matched in subsequent texts. It is as if de Beauvoir wishes to make amends for her mother's life, to challenge the world, as she could not challenge her father, to address the conditions of the life of a married woman. This hidden motive then made it inevitable that de Beauvoir would present such an overwhelmingly negative view of marriage and motherhood; the possibility of the positive aspects of conjugal existence was written out by the assumption that anything approaching an endorsement of marriage/motherhood was sheer mystification or refusal to acknowledge reality.

To Sartre and to de Beauvoir's parents must go the credit for making *The Second Sex* such a uniquely coherent and endlessly disturbing text. Of course de Beauvoir does her scholarly duty by reference to diverse texts and sources of evidence, but the emotional energy of the book seems drawn from two main sources: her feelings about her own family and her experience of family life, and her sense of exclusion from the male intellectual/symbolic order which was so clearly an essential part of her relationship with Sartre. Thus what *The Second Sex* can remind us of so forcefully today is the psychic wound to women of the creation and control of the symbolic and intellectual order by men. Whether or not this results from any innate capacity or need by men to dominate and order nature is less the issue (on which all readers will have their own views and positions) than the conscious and evident perception by women that knowledge is not structured in gender-free ways, but is in fact formed by a deep engagement by gender difference. To add insult to injury (or to ensure an even higher degree of male control of knowledge than might anyway be possible), the nature and content of knowledge is then presented to the world as universalistic.

Postmodernism has made possible the questioning of universalism in a way which was hardly dreamt of in 1949. It is evident from reading *The Second Sex* that de Beauvoir embraced the epistemological assumptions of universalism: far from wishing to reject many of the theories and ideas of the Western intellectual heritage, she wished to shift their relevance so that women as much as men could have the full status of human being. But what she did not question (and indeed it is only recently that such questioning has been apparent) was the epistemological status of Western philosophy. De Beauvoir did not take the step of challenging that heritage in terms of its preoccupation with the male and masculinity. For her, the goal to be achieved through philosophical relevance remained that of *universal* relevance: the possibility of the *impossibility* of this project was decades away. Even though de Beauvoir took the major step of recognising that Western philosophy was gendered, she hesitated at the implications of this and could not take the step of using that understanding as a destabilising force.

However, the step which de Beauvoir refused to take (of questioning entire epistemological systems as much as defining their omissions) has been taken by subsequent feminists.[3] In a real sense, therefore, contemporary feminism has taken the step which de Beauvoir, for all kinds of biographical and intellectual reasons, could not make – it has disempowered, or begun the project of disempowering, knowledge as a form of male control. In the context of postmodernism (not to mention a material context in the West which provides relatively effective contraception for heterosexual women, a degree of economic independence for many, and a cultural space for the discussion of women's experiences) it is possible for women to accept gender difference in a way which was problematic in 1949. Put simply, to accept the label 'woman' or 'feminine' in 1949 had both empirical and metaphorical implications which have shifted in the 1990s. 'Woman' as a term and a state of being retains much that is coercive, but coercive in a different and less immediately constricting way. De Beauvoir wrote *The Second Sex* just as France begun its rapid post-Second World War modernisation, and to write the book at that point inevitably involved de Beauvoir in a sense of radical social change. Added to that, the book was written during a period in which de Beauvoir travelled to the United States, and for the first time saw a materially affluent society replete with possible freedoms for its white middle class. It was also the point in de Beauvoir's life when she became deeply involved in the heterosexual discourse of North America; through de Beauvoir's affair with Nelson Algren, she stepped into a world of very different assumptions about marriage and sexual morality than that of bourgeois Catholic France.[4]

In Deidre Bair's biography of de Beauvoir, she tells us that early in the relationship with Algren de Beauvoir wrote to him about contraception. Bair writes:

> She was worried now because they were planning to spend several months in foreign countries and 'it would be terrible if anything happened – it must not have a single chance of happening'. Up until now, she told him, she had always asked the men to take 'care of the thing, and as they were few of them and always reliable and friendly, they always did and there was no problem for me'. (1990: 373)

In the same passage, Bair quotes de Beauvoir referring to Algren as her 'husband' and we know from the biography (and *The Mandarins*) that Algren gave de Beauvoir a ring which she was to wear until her dying day. Thus in the context of the relationship with Algren, 'ordinary' concerns and symbols of heterosexuality are spoken of. Again, from both *The Mandarins* and the testimony of *Force of Circumstance*, the sexual passion between Algren and de Beauvoir was considerable and a source of unequivocal pleasure for de Beauvoir. The point of these remarks, however, is less to remark on de Beauvoir's sexual life than to emphasise de Beauvoir's total absorption and engagement in conventional heterosexuality at the time of writing *The Second Sex*. We know from material published after de Beauvoir's death that she had women lovers, but what is striking about these affairs is that they were generally hidden, whereas (and as Algren bitterly pointed out) the relationship with Algren was publicly and joyfully reproduced. The passages in *The Mandarins* which record the de Beauvoir/Algren affair are a hymn to conventionally organised and described heterosexuality: the description de Beauvoir uses is 'my body was rising from the dead' (1979a: 421).

But as de Beauvoir found a new pleasure in heterosexuality, she also began to encounter some of the problems of its social organisation. Algren's view of sexual relations was clearly far more conventional than that of Sartre. First, he assumed that two people as committed to each other as he and de Beauvoir were should live, if not together, then at least on the same side of the Atlantic. He also assumed that commitment implied 'forsaking all others'. Recognising that the relationship between de Beauvoir and Sartre had long since ceased to be physically expressive, he found it hard to understand the nature of the ties between them. Thus two understandings, of commitment, and of sexuality and fidelity, began to surface and were eventually to bring the relationship to an unhappy end. However, the nature of the struggle between the two remains very much part of *The Second Sex* and of de Beauvoir's work. If one fairly explicit subtext of *The Second Sex* is de Beauvoir's fury at her exclusion from the intellectual world, and her intention to use the forms and practices of masculinity in order to enter it, then another subtext is the powerful sense of heterosexual desire which the text communicates. The chapter on 'The Lesbian', while it includes some irrefutable validations of female homosexual experience, also makes the point that (at least in the view of de Beauvoir) women involved in sexual relationships with each other are 'pitiless towards each other'. De Beauvoir continues:

> they thwart, provoke, pursue, fall upon one another tooth and nail, and drag each other down into bottomless abjection. Masculine imperturbability, whether due to indifference or self-control, is a barrier against which feminine scenes break in vain like swirling waters against a dike; but between two women tears and frenzies rise in alternate crescendo; their appetite for outdoing each other in reproaches and for endlessly 'having it out' is insatiable. Demands, recriminations, jealousy, tyrannizing – all these plagues of married life are here let loose with redoubled intensity. (1964b: 395)

We know, from the diaries and letters published after de Beauvoir's death, that she had many fraught relationships with women. *The Prime of Life* and *Force of Circumstance* both include accounts of the problems which de Beauvoir encountered in her relations with women – problems that can be seen as generally related to the problem of similarity. That is, that in her relations with Olga, Lise, Wanda et al., de Beauvoir found herself confronted by being of the same sex and with many of the same experiences. Thus the absence of difference (and the other woman's marked lack of interest in de Beauvoir's intellectual competence) made the relationships consistently difficult. Because women had little or no respect for the very skills which de Beauvoir had so assiduously acquired, skills of the male world of the intellect and rationality, she was faced in these relationships with acute questions of being: of defining herself in more fundamental terms than those of academic skill. In relations with men, on the other hand, her very difference from the majority of women made it possible for her to maintain a degree of independence and control. That this had always been the case prior to her relationship with Algren is evident from her auto-biography and *She Came to Stay*; the shift which the relationship with Algren involved was a shift away *from* the unconventional *to* the conventional. The sexual freedoms de Beauvoir and Sartre allowed each other, together with the bonds of a fierce intellectual partnership, were replaced by expectations, on Algren's side, of a faithful marriage or quasi-marriage. De Beauvoir clearly colluded with Algren's expectations, in that she addressed him as 'husband' and spoke of their 'marriage'.

This episode, and de Beauvoir's descriptions of the relationship, is problematic in the light of feminist readings of her work as explicitly and consciously committed to the independence and autonomy of women and a challenge to the patriarchal order. In a recent (1992) edition of *Signs*, a number of feminist writers argued – as Judith Butler had done in *Gender Trouble* – that de Beauvoir went a considerable way to maintaining the separation of sex and gender.[5] Butler had argued that in *The Second Sex*:

> Beauvoir is clear that one 'becomes' a woman, but always under a cultural compulsion to become one. And clearly, the compulsion does not come from 'sex'. There is nothing in her account that guarantees that the 'one' who becomes a woman is necessarily female. If 'the body is a situation', as she claims, there is no recourse to a body that has not

always already been interpreted by cultural meanings; hence, sex could not qualify as a prediscursive anatomical facticity. Indeed, sex, by definition, will be shown to have been gender all along. (Butler, 1990: 8)

What Butler is doing here (and in the subsequent discussion in *Gender Trouble*) is moving de Beauvoir towards a social constructionist account of femininity. At the same time, there is another, more radical argument at work:

Although Beauvoir is often understood to be calling for the right of women, in effect, to become existential subjects and, hence, for inclusion within the terms of an abstract universality, her position also implies a fundamental critique of the very disembodiment of the abstract masculine epistemological subject. (Butler, 1990: 11)

Throughout her account of de Beauvoir, Butler is quite correctly drawing attention to certain crucial aspects of *The Second Sex*: de Beauvoir's account of gender as a construction (thus opening up, as Butler points out, the possibility that individuals of either sex can construct themselves as feminine), and her attack on the universalism of 'the abstract masculine epistemological subject'. Yet at the same time as de Beauvoir does much in *The Second Sex* which is innovative, what might be described as the seductiveness of masculinity remains. It remains in one clearly apparent sense in de Beauvoir's impassioned concluding remarks about the claims of women to autonomy. Equally, it remains in another sense: that of the female body as one which is most likely to find fulfilment in heterosexuality. Of course de Beauvoir rails against the constraints on female sexuality. Most women in France in 1949 probably shared her view. But what makes her account differ from that of later feminists in her own country (particularly Irigaray and Wittig) is that she does not entertain the idea of *compulsory* heterosexuality. Running like a silver thread through *The Second Sex* is the implicit assumption that heterosexual desire is normal, if badly constructed and inadequately organised. Hence the contention above that in their different ways Sartre and Algren provide the core biographical experiences of *The Second Sex*: the one validated de Beauvoir's epistemological system and the second shared with her the experience of a validation of 'normal' heterosexuality. The problem with this 'normal' heterosexuality was that it had echoes of the mind/body split which was characteristic of so much of the post-Enlightenment philosophy in which de Beauvoir had been educated. De Beauvoir had shared a sexual life with Sartre (and was a voyeuristic presence in that part of his sexual life which did not include her) and Algren was an accomplished and successful novelist. Neither man was simply one half of the mind/body equation. Nevertheless, each represented a different form of the possible forms of masculine presence and indeed power. In the descriptions of sexuality in *The Second Sex*, what is striking is how similar the passages are to those in *The Mandarins* in which de Beauvoir describes, in fictional terms, her affair with Algren. In none of these passages is there a hint of the subversion of gender identity which Butler, and others, suggest. Indeed, what is striking about the descriptions is the absolutely conventional tone in which they are written. Thus, for example, this description of heterosexuality in *The Second Sex*:

> Sex pleasure in woman, as I have said, is a kind of magic spell; it demands complete abandon; if words or movements oppose the magic of caresses, the spell is broken . . . [Woman] would abolish all sur- roundings, abolish the singularity of the moment, of herself, and of her lover, she would fain be lost in a carnal night as shadowy as the mater- nal womb . . . As we have seen, she wants to remain subject while she is made object. Being more profoundly beside herself than is man because her whole body is moved by desire and excitement, she retains her subjectivity, only through union with her partner. (1964b: 372)

and in *The Mandarins*:

> I kissed his eyes, his lips, my mouth send down along his chest. His smell, his warmth made me dizzy as with drink and I felt my life leaving me, my old life with its worries, its weariness, its worn-out memories . . . I used to value pleasure for what it was worth, but I never knew that making love could be so overwhelming. The past, the future, every- thing that was separating us died at the foot of our bed. (1979a: 435)

Both these passages make explicit the possible delights of heterosexuality; in both contexts de Beauvoir is not talking about the rewards of sexual relationships between two beings of inde- terminate gender. She is quite clearly speaking of sexual relations between women and men, in which articulated sexual difference is part of the attraction (the descriptions of Lewis Brogan in *The Mandarins* are replete with references to his conventional mas- culinity and his physical competence). Therefore to argue, as

Butler and others do, that de Beauvoir disturbs categories of gender, is only part of the case. Inevitably, in examining accepted understandings of femininity de Beauvoir criticises taken-for-granted wisdom. Yet, at the same time, there runs through *The Second Sex* (and much of her work) a rich vein of the affirmation of conventional masculinity. As Toril Moi has pointed out, this has enraged and fascinated many critics:

> [de Beauvoir] is either idealised as the perfect feminist who could do nothing wrong . . . [or] that Simone de Beauvoir betrayed her feminism all along . . . It is interesting in itself that there are such widely opposing views of de Beauvoir. I suspect that none of them is quite right. (1994: 109)

What Moi proposes for her own study of de Beauvoir is a focus on 'the intellectual woman', and she writes that, 'Beauvoir is always preoccupied with the problems of knowing: knowing oneself, the other and the world' (1994: 7). Her project proposes an investigation into what Moi describes as 'knowledge' in de Beauvoir; an explicit and welcome work, even if it ignores the not inconsiderable problem regarding de Beauvoir, that one area she manifestly did *not* wish to investigate too closely was herself, others and individual motivation. She very obviously wished to construct a coherent account of her life (the project of the woman-as-author which she identified in *Memoirs of a Dutiful Daughter* as the ambition of her adolescence), but what this coherent account was seldom allowed to include was the views of others. Knowledge certainly, but the partiality and incompleteness of that knowledge was its very cornerstone.

In terms of de Beauvoir's relationship to feminism, therefore, we are left with a woman whose life and work, like that of many towering and mythical figures, defies and denies definition and annexation. From the point of view of radical feminism, it is clearly unsatisfactory to have in de Beauvoir an iconographic figure who embraced masculinity both literally and metaphorically. From the point of view of those who prefer their intellectuals to be coherent and uncontradictory, de Beauvoir is equally unsatisfactory. Refusing a great deal of what she could have known, she nevertheless constructed an account of gender relations which remains disturbing and powerful. *The Second Sex* (and much of de

Beauvoir's work) remains fascinating precisely because it is an 'unstable' text. Its very lack of coherence, its frequent contradictions and numerous equivocations, constitute a picture of reality from which subsequent generations of feminists have been able to seek sustenance. As a feminist 'mother', de Beauvoir more than met the implications of that role – she provided both emotional and intellectual sustenance for that majority of women who live within precisely those contradictions which we daily experience.

Notes

1. Simone de Beauvoir's *The Second Sex* was first published in 1949 in two volumes as *Le Deuxième Sexe*. An English translation (by Howard Parshley) was published in 1953 by Alfred Knopf, but this translation (on which all subsequent editions are based) has been widely criticised. See the discussion by Terry Keefe (1993: 19) and the account in Deidre Bair (1990: 432–7, 663–4).

2. This is stated explicitly by de Beauvoir in an interview in 1979; see Sonia Kruks (1992: 96).

3. See, for example, the work of Sandra Harding and others cited in Gunew (1990).

4. Elaine Tyler May in *Great Expectations* (1980), gives an account of the very different North American assumptions about marriage and sexuality from those of Europe.

5. See special 'cluster' on de Beauvoir in *Signs*, vol. 18, no. 1, Autumn 1992.

4

The Personal and the Political

One of the great slogans of feminism in the early 1970s was 'the personal is political'. What the slogan very effectively did was to challenge the idea that the domestic space is a private one, and that what occurs therein is of no public concern. For women living in violent relationships with men, for children and adolescents who are the subject of sexual abuse, and for people of either sex whose domestic lives are a misery, the concept of the inviolability of the domestic world imprisons them in a world in which the public cannot intervene. Thus the feminism of the 1970s and 1980s brought about, in North America and Western Europe, a shift in the assumptions of the public world about the extent to which it could legitimately intervene in the home. As a result, public attitudes towards domestic violence, rape in marriage and the sexual abuse of children began, very slowly, to change.

The point of these remarks about the public and private and its relationship to feminism in the context of a discussion of de Beauvoir is that de Beauvoir belonged to a generation in which the lines between the public and the private were drawn in ways which have now been transformed. De Beauvoir, as we have seen, wrote both extensively and highly selectively about her 'private' life. It was not until the last years of her life that she began to examine

Sartre and her relationship with him in the light of general patterns of gender relations.[1] For de Beauvoir, the 'public' was constructed in the tradition of classic Western liberalism, the arena of the state (and for government), political parties and institutional political action. Throughout the Second World War, the 1950s and the 1960s, de Beauvoir took a considerable (and at times considerably hazardous and considerably courageous) part in formal political life. Only in the 1970s, as feminism began to develop a politics and, more important, a form of politics of its own, did de Beauvoir begin to examine the boundaries in her own life between the private and the public. Indeed, it is only in the final volume of her auto-biography *(All Said and Done)* that de Beauvoir, in her discussion of her dreams, allows the reader explicit access to her 'inner' world.

De Beauvoir was brought up in a household where politics, in the sense of formal political allegiances, were discussed. De Beauvoir grew up knowing about her parent's political affiliations; the house-hold was not one in which politics remained a secret of the ballot box. De Beauvoir's father had ultra-conservative views about politics; for example, he regarded the eventual acquittal and rehabilitation of Dreyfus as a failure of the French state, rather than as a victory for those opposed to anti-Semitism. His thinking about domestic life was as conservative as his thinking about public life; the duty of the wife was to serve and entertain the husband, and children owed their parents (particularly their father) blind and absolute obedience.

But Georges de Beauvoir was not, of course, the only parent in de Beauvoir's life. Most biographers give the political views of Françoise de Beauvoir little or no attention. The classic statement about the politics of de Beauvoir's parents is that de Beauvoir was born to 'middle class parents, and her father was a lawyer of con-servative views'. Yet to say of a man who seriously believed that the verdict in the Dreyfus case should *not* have been challenged that he is 'conservative' is extending the limits of the term beyond conven-tional understanding. Given that de Beauvoir *père* had these views, there is all the more reason to look for different interpretations of the political world in the de Beauvoir household. It is then that the part of Françoise de Beauvoir becomes so crucial in constructing de Beauvoir's own understanding of politics and gender difference. Very little – as suggested above – is written about Françoise de

Beauvoir's ideas about formal politics. The consensus among biographers of de Beauvoir, and by de Beauvoir herself, is that her mother had little developed interest in formal politics, but a great deal in morality and religion. Belief in God was a matter of consistent dispute between Georges and Françoise. For Françoise, belief in God was central to her life, and God defined in strictly Roman Catholic terms. Georges was an equally convinced non-believer, who nevertheless tolerated his wife's attempts to instil into his daughters a belief in God as fervent and as dogmatic as her own.

The differences in opinion between her parents exposed de Beauvoir, and indeed any reader of her life, to a series of complex questions about the nature of politics and indeed politics in the household. One reading of this particular family is that only Georges had an interest in 'politics'. Yet that reading now looks redundant, and indeed anachronistic, in the light of what feminism has taught us to recognise about the nature of 'politics'. Politics in the informal sense – of endless, everyday, decisions and choices made in the light of general theories – has now acquired a recognised existence, and an important area in which the publicly powerless (most centrally women) demonstrate their ability to order and control their immediate world. Women in France could not even vote until after the Second World War, but it is apparent from the number of independent women who people the pages of de Beauvoir's autobiography that women in pre-1945 France were very far from powerless in any absolute sense. The idea of women's influence has rightly been questioned by feminists (who see in it a potentially legitimating gloss on women's lack of public, institutional power), but it is clear from reading de Beauvoir that she was deeply, and significantly, affected by her mother's independence of thought. What we therefore have, in the case of de Beauvoir as for millions of other women, is a model of a determined and independently minded woman living within the context of an entirely conventional marriage. The content of Françoise de Beauvoir's thought obviously infuriated and horrified her daughter; witness this comment in *A Very Easy Death*:

> She could not discuss her difficulties with anyone at all, not even herself. She had not been taught to see her own motives plainly nor to use her own judgement. She had to take shelter behind authority: but the

authorities she respected were not in agreement; there was hardly a single point in common between the Mother Superior of Les Oiseaux and my father. I had experienced this setting of one idea against another while my mind was being formed and not after it was set: thanks to my early childhood I had a confidence in myself that my mother did not possess in the least: the road of argument, disputation – my road – was closed to her. On the contrary, she had made up her mind to share the general opinion: the last person who spoke to her was right . . . In her last years she did attain some kind of coherence in her ideas, but at the time when her emotional life was at its most tormented she possessed no doctrine, no concepts, no words with which to rationalise her situation. (1965b: 38)

What this comment reveals is as much about the daughter as the mother. The last lines in particular speak of de Beauvoir's own life-long pattern of rationalising emotional life, and frequently being disturbed by those events which did not immediately lend themselves to her rational understanding. De Beauvoir learned to rationalise, and indeed acquired a mastery of rational thought and rational systems of thought. All this was part of her academic and intellectual education. But at the same time she acquired from her mother an understanding of a person's capacity for grim determination. In the steely, single-minded attitude in which the adolescent de Beauvoir approached her studies and her emancipation from the conservative Catholicism of her family, she entirely mirrored her mother's behaviour. Just as Françoise de Beauvoir hung on to her marriage and to maintaining a public face of a united married couple, so her daughter set her face against all obstacles and literally studied her way into the world which she wished to enter. Despite the constant evidence of Georges' repeated infidelity. Françoise defended her husband and consistently acted the part of the wife in a stable marriage.

The cost of this endless self-deception and refusal to acknowledge emotional pain was considerable. Her daughter was to write after her mother's death that:

Cut off from the pleasures of the body, deprived of the satisfactions of vanity, tied down to wearisome tasks that bored and humiliated her, this proud and obstinate woman did not possess the gift of resignation. Between her fits of anger she was perpetually singing, gossiping, making jokes, drowning her heart's complaints with noise. When, after my father's death, Aunt Germaine hinted that he had not been an ideal husband, Maman snubbed her fiercely. 'He always made me very happy.' And certainly that was what she always told herself! (1965b: 34)

These sentences were written in 1964; only one year before de Beauvoir had herself written, in the conclusion to *Force of Circumstance*, that 'There has been one undoubted success in my life: my relationship with Sartre' (1965a: 643). In that same important conclusion, de Beauvoir makes much of the symbiotic quality of her relationship with Sartre, and equally the extent to which she chose the relationship and was always in full agreement with him. What de Beauvoir also goes to some lengths to explain is her view of her intellectual standing in relationship to Sartre. Since the passage runs counter to many contemporary accounts of de Beauvoir, it is worth quoting in full:

> This does not alter the fact that philosophically and politically the initiative has always come from him. Apparently some young women have felt let down by this fact; they took it to mean that I was accepting the 'relative' role I was advising them to escape from. No. Sartre is ideologically creative, I am not; this bent forced him into making political choices and going much more profoundly into the reasons for them than I was interested in doing. The real betrayal of my liberty would have been a refusal to recognise this particular superiority on his part; I would then have ended up a prisoner of the deliberately challenging attitude and the bad faith which are at once an inevitable result of the battle of the sexes and the complete opposite of intellectual honesty. My independence has never been in danger because I have never unloaded any of my own responsibilities onto Sartre. I have never given my support to any idea, any decision, without first having analysed it and accepted it on my own account. My emotions have been the product of a direct contact with the world. My own work has demanded from me a great many decisions and struggles, a great deal of research, perseverance and hard work. He has helped me, as I have helped him. I have not lived through him. (1965a: 645)

But critics of de Beauvoir would differ from this view. Kate Fullbrook and Edward Fullbrook, Michèle de Doeuff, Toril Moi and others (many of whom were writing in the 1980s) all argue that de Beauvoir was an extremely original thinker, and in fact a far more original thinker than Sartre (see Fullbrook and Fullbrook, 1993; le Doeuff, 1987). Even if we regard this issue of 'who is more original' as part of a tedious academic game, what remains are the assertions and protestations by de Beauvoir which we have to set against a now substantial critical literature. Thus her final sentence above – 'I have not lived through him' – appears a particularly sensitive denial; nobody at that point (that is, 1963) had claimed that de Beauvoir *had* lived through Sartre. In 1963 the secondary literature on de Beauvoir was almost non-existent, and certainly no one in print had claimed that de Beauvoir was a mere cipher of Sartre.

But by the 1990s there *is* a substantial literature on de Beauvoir, and a great deal more is known about the 'private' lives of both Sartre and de Beauvoir. De Beauvoir, certainly by 1963, was well on the way to becoming a figure of global fame. In the 1950s this fame was constructed through the publication of *The Second Sex, The Mandarins* and the first volumes of autobiography, as well as de Beauvoir's increasing involvement in public politics. The crucial involvement which this involved was over the issue of decolonisation in French Algeria (the French government of the 1950s attempted to maintain direct French rule, and opposed the construction of an Algerian national state). Later, in the 1960s, both Sartre and de Beauvoir were to join the international opposition to United States policy in Vietnam. Thus by the end of the 1960s de Beauvoir was established not just as a feminist, but as a feminist who identified with left-wing, radical, politics.

This brief summary of de Beauvoir's involvement does scant justice to the time and energy which she gave in the 1950s and 1960s to unpopular political causes, in which (certainly in the case of opposition to French policy in Algeria) she ran the risk of possible assassination and certain public hostility. The point of the summary, however, is to attest to de Beauvoir's willingness (and increasing willingness as she grew older) to become involved in public politics – the kind of politics which are conventionally recognised as such. In this, she did not have to challenge Sartre (since his political views very closely matched hers), and so did not have to maintain a political path in opposition to her partner. Thus far she was unlike her mother, in that for her there were no central differences of opinion at this point about the public world.

But as the 1960s wore on, and particularly as a vocal and vehement feminism emerged which increasingly began to challenge the definition of the term 'politics', so de Beauvoir's political stance, and her relationship to Sartre, began to shift. The words which she wrote so confidently in 1963 – 'In more than thirty years, we have only once gone to sleep at night disunited' – began to look increasingly empty as politics – both public and private – began to shift and in so doing brought about transformations in the de Beauvoir/Sartre relationship. Crucial among these shifts was Sartre's political involvement with Maoism, and in particular the figure of Benny Lévy.[2] As these shifts occurred, what became apparent – again – was how much de Beauvoir had absorbed in her childhood from her mother's strength and determination. The cracks which had appeared in the 1940s between de Beauvoir and Sartre (over Sartre's involvement with Dolores Vanetti) were now as nothing compared with the divisions created between the couple by Sartre's espousal of Maoism, his adoption as his daughter of Arlette Elkaïm, and his increasing physical debilitation. 'We cannot escape childhood' it is often said; the remark frequently has the tone of threat and fatalism about it, but for de Beauvoir the sense of power acquired in childhood was not to be a threat in adult life, but a resource and a strength in the last 20 years of her life.

Thus as de Beauvoir became increasingly energised by the feminism of the late 1960s and the early 1970s, so she turned her attention – her public political attention – to the public examination of personal and 'private' life. The old boundaries of the 1940s and the 1950s (boundaries which had been maintained not just by de Beauvoir but by an entire European generation) began to dissolve, and we find de Beauvoir increasingly inclined to examine *some* of the previously 'private' areas of her life. What this means in effect is that she turns her attention to Sartre and to the nature of their relationship. In a series of interviews and discussions, she questioned Sartre about his attitude to women and his position vis-à-vis 'the woman question'. These interviews (published collectively in *Adieux*) suggest that de Beauvoir has learned a new vocabulary and understanding from feminism, a vocabulary which includes the explicit recognitions of power relations between women and men. It is not that de Beauvoir suddenly discovered in the 1960s the idea that men and women struggled for their own interpretation of events (the author of *She Came to Stay* was clearly well aware that relationships between the sexes frequently include disputes over definitions and decisions), but what she did now use was a newly created language about sexual exploitation and oppression.

In the way which was typical of her engagement with the world, de Beauvoir codified her increasing engagement with feminism through the means of her writing. The particular vehicle for this codification (as *Memoirs of a Dutiful Daughter* had effectively 'organised' de Beauvoir's escape from home, and *The Prime of Life* 'organised' the early years of the relationship with Sartre) was *All Said and Done*, the final volume of de Beauvoir's autobiography which was published in 1972 (1979c). Deidre Bair has noted that throughout the 1960s many people were urging de Beauvoir to engage with emergent feminism. Bair writes:

> By 1966 the continuing question of her feminism or the lack thereof became too strong for Beauvoir to ignore. Francis Jeanson expressed the charge best when he accused her of understanding the feminine condition only because she had escaped from it. She denied this, claiming she had never written condescendingly of women but had only depicted their true position in society. She insisted that 'the only interpretations of my feminism that are false in my eyes are those that are not *radically* feminist. One never falsifies my views in drawing me toward absolute feminism.' (1990: 546)

This statement is interesting in that it contains what appears to be a fervent commitment to radical feminism and with it a form of analysis of gender relations which de Beauvoir was elsewhere to deny. For most readers of feminism, the term 'radical feminism' carries with it the understanding of essential differences between women and men – it is the theoretical territory of writers such as Kate Millett, Mary Daly and Monique Wittig. Equally, the term 'absolute' feminism suggests a view of the world in which a feminist understanding is *the* central form of understanding of the social world, and as such a priority which is more important than socialist or Marxist analysis.

Exactly what de Beauvoir meant by her remarks about feminism led her, in the 1970s, into a number of complex debates and differences with French feminists. In this, what emerged was the deeply problematic nature of *The Second Sex*. It is apparent from all de Beauvoir's writing and her public statements that she would like to emerge as a consistent and coherent thinker and human being. What is equally apparent is that *The Second Sex* is a text which can be read in diverse ways, as can de Beauvoir's other writing and the events of her life. When de Beauvoir said, as an adolescent, that she wanted her life 'to be a beautiful story', she did not allow for the possibilities of compromise and inconsistency which make up the majority of lives. One reading of de Beauvoir is therefore that she spent her life attempting to fit her views and her actions (particularly her actions in terms of her relations with others) into a firmly constructed template. Having made up her mind what her life would be like, she then remained deeply attached to the idea of the organisation of her actions to fit this theoretical construction. The Second World War was the first event which shook the social security of de Beauvoir's life. Eventually, de Beauvoir found a way of adapting to these events, and to integrating them into her life-pattern. Sartre's affair with Dolores Vanetti again threatened de Beauvoir's pattern of life, and finally so did feminism.

Of these various threats and challenges to de Beauvoir's world, arguably the most serious challenge was that of feminism. Unlike the other disturbing events in which boundaries between public and private were firmly maintained, feminism was – and is – organised around two central themes: that it is impossible, and even undesirable, to maintain distinctions between the public and the private, and that universalistic epistemologies are inappropriate to the understanding of the situation of women. On the second theme, de Beauvoir was on firm ice, given that *The Second Sex* is an attack on the very idea that the human condition is uniquely a masculine condition. But on the former theme, the dissolution of the boundaries between the public and private, de Beauvoir was on very much thinner ice, not least because her private world was one which she explicitly shared with a man, and because she energetically maintained through her autobiography an impressive official and public history of her life.

Throughout de Beauvoir's life it is striking that she always maintains one person as her central, intimate 'other', even though she may well be engaged in other, apparently intimate, relationships at the same time. Elaine Marks (1973) argues that this pattern (first, the 'twin' relationship with ZaZa – Elisabeth le Coin – then the relationship with Sartre and finally the friendship with Sylvie le Bon) is part of de Beauvoir's life-long fear of death and the destruction of the ego. Drawing on an essay by Freud written in 1919, Elaine

Marks argues that the notion of 'the double' who saves the individual from death is particularly strong in the case of Sylvie le Bon. De Beauvoir describes the relationship in *All Said and Done* thus:

> The better I knew Sylvie, the more akin I felt to her. She too was an intellectual and she too was passionately in love with life. And she was like me in many other ways: with thirty three years of difference I recognised my qualities and my faults in her . . . She is as thoroughly interwoven in my life as I am in hers. I have introduced her to my friends. We read the same books, we see shows together, and we go for long drives in the car. There is such an interchange between us that I lose the sense of my age: she draws me forwards into her future, and there are times when the present recovers a dimension that it had lost. (quoted in Marks, 1973: 199)

And so through Sylvie de Beauvoir is protected against death, against that fear of the destruction of the ego which Freud had identified.

We can, therefore, allow Sylvie le Bon (and Sartre and Elisabeth le Coin) a place in de Beauvoir's life-long engagement with the fear and the allure of death. All these individuals promised the existence of an external world to the self, and an external world which would survive the death of the other party. The three figures overlap with each other in the chronology of de Beauvoir's life: as Elisabeth dies, so de Beauvoir begins the relationship with Sartre, and as Sartre begins his long and painful death (and dies to de Beauvoir metaphorically, if not literally, through his friendship with Arlette Elkaïm), so de Beauvoir develops the relationship with Sylvie. The dynamic of de Beauvoir's emotional life is therefore one in which *an* other always plays a crucial and sustaining part. It is also impossible to avoid noting that two of the three 'others' are women and, even though Sartre was male, his masculinity (not least by his own account) was very much constructed through his relations with women rather than with men. Part of the attraction of Sartre for de Beauvoir was his difference from many aspects of conventional masculinity: with Sartre de Beauvoir could be the more physically active partner (the passionately enthusiastic walker and cyclist of their youth), and with him too she could display intellectual aggression and sexual promiscuity without fear of conventional displays of disapproval for such unseemly behaviour by a woman. Secure in his success in one aspect of conventional masculinity, Sartre could offer to de Beauvoir a *private* public place in which to explore and test her assumptions about the world.

So for many years Sartre was in a sense de Beauvoir's public world. The need for a male figure who constitutes the public world can be seen in various ways; within psychoanalysis Lacan's discussions of a mirror stage, and Freud's, and Freudian, hypotheses about the development of female sexuality all have a resonance in the case of de Beauvoir. Before her death we knew (for a long time largely because she told us) that Sartre was the central 'other'; he was to her the witness to her life, just as much as she was to his. After her death, and particularly after the publication of de Beauvoir's letters to Sartre, it is possible to see more of the nature of the relationship and de Beauvoir's own construction of Sartre as her mirror and as her public. For example, in the following extracts from her letters to Sartre, de Beauvoir tells him of her night with Wanda (also a lover of Sartre's) and – in the second extract – reassures Sartre that her affair with Algren is over. She writes thus to Sartre about Wanda:

> We returned to her place, went to bed and talked a bit, then moved on to embraces. I found it really charming to sleep in her room like that, though I slept quite badly since she shifts around and snores – which is just like her. We woke up at about 8.30, and like a satisfied man I avoided her caresses. I wanted to have breakfast and work (I feel I can get right into your skin at such moments). (1991: 218)

and to Sartre about Algren:

> At any rate don't worry about me, since I know that in three months we'll be together again; and that you're my life; and that I can't regret this affair being dead, since its death was implied in the life I've chosen – which you give me. Goodbye, my dear little one. Do write. Extract yourself as best you can from your own troubles. (1991: 460)

About these extracts it must be said, first, that de Beauvoir knew (and Sartre knew that de Beauvoir knew) that Wanda and Sartre had had a sexual relationship. Being in bed with Wanda is therefore quite literally following Sartre. Second, in 1950, when de Beauvoir wrote to Sartre about the 'death' of her affair with Nelson Algren, she was also telling Algren about her commitment to him and addressing him as 'husband'. However elastic and negotiable the term may have been in 1950 (or is now), it is apparent that Algren understood the term, and de Beauvoir used it, to imply a life-long commitment. Third, there are characteristic structures in the letter from de Beauvoir to Sartre quoted above: the use of the diminutive 'little'/*petit* to address Sartre, the denial of the importance of de Beauvoir's relations with others when compared with the relationship with Sartre and the promise/ threat to Sartre that he is her 'life'. Having told Sartre that the affair is dead and that he is the important figure in her life, she then completes the square of her emotional pattern by encouraging Sartre to end his relationship with Dolores Vanetti. Further, Dolores is reduced to the status of 'troubles', the implication being that Sartre, like de Beauvoir, can certainly deal with this problematic, if necessary, interlude.[3]

The letters from de Beauvoir to Sartre were not – we have to assume – written for publication, and we know from evidence which emerged after de Beauvoir's death that she went out of her way during her lifetime to suppress their publication. Obviously, there were numerous reasons for this: a perfectly credible desire to protect the privacy of others (Sylvie le Bon, for example, is still alive at the time of writing) and an equally credible recognition that the letters, not to mention the actions which they describe, do not always reflect well on de Beauvoir. It is not just that a public world might pass moral judgement on de Beauvoir (which sections of French society had already done anyway), but that questions would be raised about the very nature of de Beauvoir's life – a life constructed by its author as a life of freedom and choice could equally well be read as a life of constraint and dependence. Again, it is not necessary to look far to find theoretical discussions of de Beauvoir's life which cast quite another light on her actions and psychoanalysis in particular is illuminating here. First, Janet Sayers describing Lacan's theory of the mirror image:

> On the other hand, Lacan's theory of the mirror stage is useful in so far as it provides a means of explaining why we are so easily duped into falsely believing that the freedom promised us by our society's ideology of individualism is already ours. For this theory draws attention to the ease with which we are captivated into believing that we are already one with any image, including that of our individual freedom, which presents as a reflection of ourselves. (1985: 85)

and second Louise Kaplan outlining Freud's theory of infantile sexuality:

A female's *forbidden* masculine wishes have the same disastrous impact
on her life as the analogous forbidden feminine wishes have on the life
of a male ... they [women] do suffer from the sense that they had
something once – powers, ambitions, longings that they had regarded
as intrinsic to the little person they were – and that their precious trea-
sures were stolen away. (1991: 82)

Both writers, and many others in the psychoanalytical traditions to
which they refer, discuss ideas which are exactly captured in de
Beauvoir's behaviour. De Beauvoir's agenda in life was to create
her own version of reality, but in doing so what was essential – for
general reasons – was a male other, both to represent an image of
freedom and to make good the symbolic loss of physical masculinity in infancy. De Beauvoir could not be a man, but what she
could do – and in fact did – was to externalise forbidden aspirations
to masculinity through the person of Sartre.

Small wonder, then, that Sartre is always 'little'. Sartre was (and
putting this in politically correct terms is a challenge of the 1990s)
not a tall man, but, apart from his literal 'little-ness', to address
him consistently as little has the effect both of infantalising him and
of placing him securely within the realms of childhood. 'Little'
Sartre could therefore represent all that de Beauvoir was not
allowed to represent for herself. He formed an essential part of de
Beauvoir's construction of herself, that masculine self which could
allow the female person to be creative and to make safe address to
the public world. Over and again in her account of her life in the
1940s and 1950s, de Beauvoir makes plain her unwillingness to
enter the public world for herself. If Sartre is involved in political
campaigns, then she is assured of being there as well. During the
war years, much of de Beauvoir's involvement was limited; *The
Prime of Life* contains many examples (as the following) which
suggest that the mother of feminism played an entirely domestic
part in political activity at this time:

Sartre went back with Salacrou to the Comédie-Française, which was
now occupied by the C.N.Th. He spent the night and all the following
day there, while I was trudging hither and thither round Paris: there
were always provisions to be hunted for somewhere or other, and I
believe I also took the first instalment of Sartre's report on the
Liberation to Camus. (1962a: 596)

and:

Now that I had had a book published, it would have been quite in order for me to attend meetings of the C.N.E., but I was put off doing so by a scruple which often subsequently made me hold back in a similar way. I was so completely in harmony with Sartre's views that my presence would simply have duplicated his, to no useful purpose. To go also struck me as both inopportune and ostentatious. It was not other people's malice I feared so much as my own embarrassment: I would have felt, in my inner heart, that I was making a tactless exhibition of myself. This criticism might not have applied if I had been in a position to accompany Sartre to C.N.E. meetings right from the beginning; and I am sure I would have managed to get there if the sessions had held any real attraction for me; but, *Sartre regarded them as a great bore!* (1962a: 563)

The italics are mine, and are there to emphasise the absolutely explicit demonstration here that de Beauvoir regarded Sartre as the public world and as her source of understanding of it. Reading the passage today, it is almost inconceivable that a woman with any measure of identification with feminism could write it; to substitute so clearly a man's voice (and authority) for a woman's is now contrary to all that is expected of women and their sense of personal autonomy. But what is also raised here is the question of the 'voice' of de Beauvoir: in what sense did she express her own views, or how far did she write to please, to entertain, to seduce and – perhaps most centrally – to retain Sartre? In the past 20 years it has become generally recognised that for women it is often difficult to negotiate a relationship with both the form and the content of the written word. The 'law of the father' which dominates the symbolic order of language remains a crucial issue in feminist writing. In the case of de Beauvoir, we have an exceptional instance of a great woman writer whose identification with, and negotiation with, masculinity was not merely (sic) symbolic but also literal. 'In the beginning was the Word, and the Word was with God', St. John's Gospel reminds and warns us. By the same token, and within the same Judeo-Christian tradition, de Beauvoir entered the intellectual world through the Word, which was with Jean-Paul Sartre.

Departing from the thrall of the authority of Sartre was to occupy much of de Beauvoir's adult life, and it is impossible not to observe here that de Beauvoir's friendship with Sylvie le Bon developed very rapidly after the death of Françoise de Beauvoir. Bair explains:

> Sylvie came back to Paris in the fall of 1963, during Françoise de Beauvoir's final illness. Her first meeting with Beauvoir took place one dismal afternoon in the same Café Raspail Vert, but this time the conversation was different, Sylvie remembered. 'We still barely knew each other when her mother died, but I remember that this day she told me virtually word for word what became the story for *A Very Easy Death*. I remembered she would stop from time to time and ask, 'What do you think? Do you think I can write that? I'd like to write that.' She needed catharsis, so I said, 'Yes, you must do it.' I suggested later that I should accompany her to the funeral, but although she was happy that I suggested it, she said no. She was right, there was no reason for me to go. At the beginning (of the renewed friendship) she was very cautious, she didn't throw herself into things. But it was her mother's death that brought us together. (1990: 507)

And it was not just that Françoise de Beauvoir's death brought Sylvie and Simone together. The friendship also served the purpose of decreasing the amount of time which de Beauvoir spent with Sartre and of shifting the pattern of priorities and allegiances within which de Beauvoir had lived her adult life. The final volume of de Beauvoir's autobiography, *All Said and Done*, is dedicated to Sylvie le Bon; a life history which began with a conventional patriarchal family life concludes with fulsome tributes to a young philosophy teacher – a teacher just like the teacher whom de Beauvoir set out to be in *Memoirs of a Dutiful Daughter*. The volumes of de Beauvoir's autobiography span a rich and varied life of 64 years, but if we concertina the years which the biography describes we find a life which begins and ends with crucial relationships with women. More curiously, *All Said and Done* ends with a discussion of de Beauvoir's atheism. Readers of the earlier autobiography would know that de Beauvoir (to her mother's horror) had lost faith in the Roman Catholic God of her childhood when she was an adolescent and this faith had never been revived. Nevertheless, the final pages of *All Said and Done* return to the subject of God. De Beauvoir discusses in these pages the nature of a child's faith in God:

> I know what a child's faith amounts to: for him believing in God
> means believing in the adults who tell him about God. When he no
> longer trusts them his faith is no more than a dubious compromise
> that consists of believing that one believes. (1979c: 497)

As she goes on to say, the study of philosophy convinced her
that belief in God was impossible. The desire to study philosophy was de Beauvoir's, but again as all readers know, it was
Jean-Paul Sartre who did much to provide her with a bridge to
familiarity and confidence with philosophical ideas. Equally, it
was the relationship with Sartre which provided, for years of
her adult life, access to the public world for de Beauvoir.

At the beginning of the final paragraph of *All Said and Done*,
de Beauvoir writes that her ambitions about writing were very
different from those of Sartre. Again, readers of those pages are
confronted by an issue which seems to spring directly from de
Beauvoir's concerns rather than the particular issues in the
text. Why, we might ask, do we need to be told that de
Beauvoir's ideas were not the same as those of Sartre? Yet we
are told first that God is dead (or at least that Simone de
Beauvoir has no faith), and then that de Beauvoir and Sartre are
separate people with different agendas. The coincidence of
these two remarks is remarkable: these final pages read like
free association rather than a structured and controlled account
of a life. But as in free association generally, more is revealed
than in the rigorously constructed text. Arguably what is
revealed here is that by 1972 (the year of the first publication of
All Said and Done) God, at least in the human personification of
Jean-Paul Sartre, was dead and de Beauvoir had recognised the
painful reality of separation and being separate. By 1972 Sartre's
domestic life (like that of de Beauvoir's) had evolved to include
a younger partner; by that date too the nature of the public
world had changed in such a way as to offer de Beauvoir,
through contemporary feminism, a central place in intellectual
history.

The final years of Sartre's life were retold in detail by de
Beauvoir in *Adieux* (1984). De Beauvoir's account of these years
(the period between 1971, when Sartre's health began to deteri-
orate seriously and his eyesight failed, and his death in 1980) is

an account which provides considerable information about the dependence on others which was forced on Sartre as a result of his physical condition. The years were plainly not happy for either party; Sartre was ill and the relationship between Sartre and de Beauvoir had become divided about Sartre's relationship with Arlette and with his 'secretary' Benny Lévy. Accounts of these years differ and will no doubt continue to differ; what has emerged is that relations between de Beauvoir and Arlette became embittered and both women made claims, after Sartre's death, to the central place in the control of the interpretation of his life and his relations with others.

It is in this light – of a need to protect and to maintain a relationship – that *Adieux* is probably best read. We can also read it as part of a shifting dynamic between Sartre and de Beauvoir in the period 1965–80. In those years de Beauvoir was perfectly content, by her own account and that of others, to hand over much of the day-to-day care and companionship of Sartre to others. She had her emerging feminist politics, Sartre had his interests in *gauchiste* politics and writing. As long as Sartre was alive, de Beauvoir remained largely confident that the relationship could be maintained: she was better informed, more skilled in debate and far more cogniscent of Sartre's thinking than any of the young people with whom Sartre surrounded himself. But the increasing problem for de Beauvoir was that just as Sartre, and the authority of other male intellectual figures, was deconstructed by feminism and postmodernism, so Sartre made considerable efforts to deconstruct himself in self-critiques and in disavowals of much of his previous work. As Sartre's intellectual work, that of post-Enlightenment rationality and humanism, started to fracture under the critique of such contemporary figures as Foucault and Baudrillard, so Sartre himself attempted to reposition himself, via radical politics, in a position of renewed historical and intellectual vitality.

Thus when de Beauvoir wrote in 1972 (at the beginning of the period of Sartre's enfeeblement) that she had no faith in God, she was in a sense expressing a double lack of faith – her own loss of faith in the project on which she and Sartre had been involved throughout their lives, and her loss of faith in

Sartre as a carrier of the central value of that project. But, and it is a very important qualification, Sartre and de Beauvoir had always been mirrors of reality, and fantasy, to each other. Just as de Beauvoir needed a male 'mirror' to provide a public world, so Sartre needed (and was used to, through his early relationship with his mother) a female mirror to sustain his private self and his sense of himself. As Bair has written of Sartre, 'All he ever wanted was to be like his childhood ideal, Pardaillon, the swash-buckling comic-book hero who was always rushing about from one adventure to another, a French Peter Pan flying forever in eternal youth' (1990: 581). For years de Beauvoir sustained this fantasy, through serious attention to his every project and willing collaboration and collusion with both his political and emotional involvements. Yet as feminism drew de Beauvoir into a public world, a public world associated with 'new' ideas and 'new' possibilities, the mirror which she had provided disappeared. Thus for both parties the sustaining re-enforcements which each had provided for the other were increasingly not there. In the midst of this shift lay the paradox of two individuals who had attempted to challenge and defy the conventional, public world now being overtaken by a public world which was, in terms of their organising ideas and assumptions, increasingly radical.

The pages of Deidre Bair's biography of de Beauvoir, like the pages of *Adieux*, which deal with the last years of Sartre and de Beauvoir do not make happy reading. Sartre became an increasingly pathetic figure, and, despite de Beauvoir's protestations that his mind remained alert until his death, there are many reasons for supposing that his illness did prevent him from coherent thought. For the second time in her life, de Beauvoir watched a person close to her die and for the second time in her life she chose not to tell that person about the nature and severity of the illness. In the case of her mother, de Beauvoir knew that she had terminal cancer but did not tell her or allow her to be told this. In the case of Sartre, de Beauvoir knew, and was told by Sartre's doctors, that when he was finally admitted to hospital he could not survive. Sartre was not told this, although his questions about the costs of his funeral suggest that he too did not expect to live. Whatever the nature of Sartre's

knowledge of his condition, de Beauvoir stood again by the bed-
side of someone whom she knew would die.

When Sartre died, de Beauvoir collapsed from the exhaustion, tension and anguish of his final days. For weeks after his
death, many people thought it likely that de Beauvoir would also
die: that life without Sartre, without the sustaining other of her
life, would not be possible. But she rallied, and spent the final six
years of her life working hard and regularly. She died almost six
years to the day after Sartre, but not before she had made further significant contributions to the history of their life together.
Adieux was one contribution, another was the collection of letters
by Sartre to de Beauvoir published in 1983 as *Lettres au Castor et
à quelques autres*. The years were also in many ways personally
happy: travel with Sylvie remained a delight and there was constant international recognition of her work.

But there was reparative work to be done. By all accounts, de
Beauvoir and Sartre had disagreed profoundly and deeply in the
months just before his death over the politics of the journal *Les
Temps Modernes*. Sartre wrote an article for the journal which
effectively challenged all his previous work. De Beauvoir was
the leader of those who advised against publication. Annie
Cohen-Solal, a biographer of Sartre, tells the tale thus:

> For the first time in their lives, they [Sartre and de Beauvoir] were
> in total disagreement. 'Sartre was never really angry,' according to
> Arlette. 'He was very solid and never lost his cool. But this time,
> after the scene with Beauvoir, he was quite ruffled. He had never
> spoken to me about any trouble with Beauvoir, but, after this crisis,
> he told me he did not understand her. Apparently, while reading the
> text, she had gotten very angry, started crying, and finally threw the
> manuscript across the room. Sartre tried to talk to her and explain
> things, but she refused to listen.
>
> Apparently, Sartre was very upset by this sudden change in his
> relationship with Beauvoir. Nor is it sure that they ever fully made up
> in the two months that separated this scene from the end of his life.
> 'I've just had lunch with those two austere muses,' he would tell
> Arlette whenever he got back from lunching with Beauvoir and a
> close friend of hers, Sylvie Le Bon. 'They did not speak to me once.'
> 'I would like to come with you two to Belle-Ile for Easter,' he told
> Sylvie on the other hand, 'and forget about that whole thing once
> and for all.' (1987: 515)

And as Cohen-Solal continues:

> He had gone against Beauvoir's wishes, he was well aware of it, and in fact, he had deliberately and obstinately taken his stance against his part, the guardians of the Temple, the Sartrean tribunal. (1987: 515)

However we read Sartre's actions and choices in the final years of his life, it is apparent that the concordat between himself and de Beauvoir had been seriously damaged, if not broken. The public – in the form of others (most significantly Lévy and Arlette) and of history – had finally broken into the private world of de Beauvoir and Sartre. Both had staked their individual lives on an engagement with history and a refusal of the conventional boundaries between public and private. Both had made of the other their public and their private world. As those worlds changed their boundaries, as the public world became more preoccupied with the private and as the private world became more public, so a relationship which had been formed in a world of certainty about public and private inevitably changed.

For de Beauvoir these shifts were both negative and positive. She had played a not insubstantial part in holding up for critical examination the public assumptions of the early twentieth century about the 'private' world of sexuality. At the same time, she had constructed for herself a public, and publicly available, account of her private life. But the expectations of the 1960s and 1970s about the knowledge of the private world changed, and as they did de Beauvoir's partial revelations, her silences and her absences all became impossible to ignore. This was not a woman writing publicly about her private life, this was a woman writing partially about aspects of her private life. In this partial account were few (if any) accounts of the feelings of others or an acknowledgement of internal motives and dynamics which may have inspired action and choice. Reading de Beauvoir in the late twentieth century, it is difficult to avoid reading her as a woman writer in the heroic tradition – a person who wished to conquer the world and was able to do so because she found in a male companion the sustaining symbolic presence which made the hero's quest for immortality possible.

86 *Simone de Beauvoir*

Notes

1. See the interviews with Alice Jardine, *Signs*, vol. 15, no. 2, Winter 1979, pp. 224–36 and with Margaret Simons in Fraser and Bartky (1992).

2. See the discussion on the importance (and disruption) of Benny Lévy in the Sartre/de Beauvoir relationship in Bair (1990: 576–7) and in Annie Cohen-Solal (1987: 498, 510–16).

3. 'Extract yourself as best you can from your own troubles' (de Beauvoir, 1991: 460).

5

Others

In this penultimate chapter the focus of my discussion is on aspects of de Beauvoir's relationships with a number of significant others in her life in relation to the broad conceptual approach developed in earlier chapters. Paramount here is the relationship with Sartre, but also more generally how de Beauvoir positioned people in relation to her (and Sartre) within her volumes of autobiography, and her friendships with Olga, Lise and a number of other women, including Sylvie le Bon, who became her adopted daughter. In her later years, feminism 'discovered' de Beauvoir and from this de Beauvoir became involved in a number of campaigns for women's rights in France. Although a detailed exploration of such involvements would be interesting in its own right, my concern is a different one; and so although the chapter does touch on these involvements, its emphasis remains very much on the nexus of significant others in de Beauvoir's life.

De Beauvoir's emancipation from her Catholic background was accomplished, as discussed earlier, with help from Sartre and friends. About this process of emancipation, there remains a great deal which can be said and/or surmised. But one interpretation, that de Beauvoir was as much misled as led by the friendship with Sartre, is neatly summed up in Adrienne Rich's poem 'Natural Resources':

The phantom of the man-who-would understand,
the lost brother, the twin –
for him did we leave our mothers.
deny our sister, over and over? (1978: 62)

For whatever reason, it is apparent that de Beauvoir's initial invest-
ment in her relationship with Sartre was considerable, and
throughout the first 10 years of their life together he remained the
central figure in her existence. Indeed, there is good reason to
argue that Sartre was always to occupy this position, and even if the
last years of his life represented a troubled time in the de
Beauvoir/Sartre relationship it is apparent that Sartre dominated
de Beauvoir's life until his death.

It did not, however, dominate de Beauvoir in ways in which the
term is often understood when applied to relationships between
women and men. He did not, for example, organise de Beauvoir's
life, control her movements or rule her friendships. She lived in her
own apartment, supported herself (and several less well-off
friends) with her own money and was involved in networks and
organisations which were quite independent of Sartre. Thus there
was no domination in the ordinary domestic sense of everyday
control and surveillance. On the other hand, what there was –
which amounted to domination of another kind – was constant concern on the part of de Beauvoir about what Sartre thought, what
Sartre was doing and whom Sartre was with. These concerns were
focused around certain key issues (Sartre's relationship with
Benny Lévy, Arlette Elkaïm and the editorial board of *Les Temps
Modernes*), but in all of them it is apparent from de Beauvoir's own
remarks and subsequent biographical information that there was
intense feeling on her part about the part that these 'others' played
in Sartre's life.

The various readings of the Sartre/de Beauvoir relationship
which are current veer between those which suggest a relationship
in which Sartre was consistently the dominant partner, with de
Beauvoir endlessly concerned about 'losing' him, to those who see
the relationship in terms of a partnership, which was constantly
renegotiated over a period of some 50 years. The former reading is
very much part of the account given by Deidre Bair of de
Beauvoir's life. Even though de Beauvoir took a considerable part

in the writing of the biography, she could not contain the impression which Bair gives of a woman who was deeply concerned about maintaining a relationship and prepared to make considerable concessions to do this. For example, Bair writes about de Beauvoir's attitude to Sartre in the years just before his death:

> part of de Beauvoir's unease stemmed from the fact that she and Sartre had not had much in common ideologically for the past several years. She was philosophically content with what he had written prior to 1955, but after that, she felt a tremendous obligation to go along with everything he espoused because of the public's perception of them as an intellectual couple. She believed her most important duty was to accompany and support him – to be seen at his side. With the exception of the Family, he and she no longer shared a common group of acquaintances. More important, they were forming individual friendships that reveal the subtly differing directions in which their lives were heading. (1990: 463)

We can hear the voice of de Beauvoir in the remark about 'she believed her most important duty'; equally, in this and other passages we can identify Bair's perception of de Beauvoir as a woman who could not leave a relationship which she had chosen in her youth. The parallel between de Beauvoir and her mother is absolutely striking; in the face of apparently conclusive evidence of her husband's carelessness and infidelity, de Beauvoir's mother persisted in maintaining publicly her belief in her marriage. She did so in the name of a conventional expectation of marriage; this was hardly the same motive in the case of her daughter, who chose to justify the relationship with Sartre in terms of shared intellectual interests. That both justifications have more than a tinge of the irrational and the religious about them is difficult to ignore; both women remained true to a particular system of belief to their dying day, and if philosophy is awarded the label of rational thought it does not decrease its irrational properties as an ingredient in de Beauvoir's emotional life.

At the other end of the continuum from readings such as Bair's is the view of Toril Moi (1994) that accounts of de Beauvoir's life with Sartre are deeply coloured by the views of her critics. Moi writes:

> Why, after the publication of her letters and diaries, are so many critics voicing their disapproval of de Beauvoir's relationship with Sartre? Beauvoir herself is partly to blame for this reaction. Although she never explicitly set her own relationship with Sartre up as an ideal for others to

follow, her writing is in fact filled with narcissistic longings for absolute
emotional fulfilment. In so far as she also writes in order to make her
readers identify with her, on her own terms her memoirs can only be
successful if they inspire the same longing in her readers. At the same
time, however, readers desperately looking for perfect (as opposed to
'good enough') role models are only too ready to fall into the psycho-
logical trap set by Beauvoir. Wanting her to be ideally happy with Sartre,
such readers project their own narcissistic ideals onto her: the pain of
having to abandon that position is what causes the recent outbursts of
disappointment, anger and rejection. The discovery of what Beauvoir's
sexual and emotional life was 'really' like makes it difficult to continue to
imagine that perfect satisfaction is to be had in this world: perhaps it is
not only Simone de Beauvoir who has some difficulty in coming to terms
with the reality principle, but her readers as well. (1994: 255)

This account (which arises in part out of Angela Carter's question 'Why is a nice girl like Simone wasting her time sucking up to
a boring old fart like Jean-Paul?') is one which gives a greater
priority than Bair's to the appeal of Sartre's mind in explaining his
continued attraction for de Beauvoir (Moi, 1994: 252). Bair (and
Bair ghosted by de Beauvoir) is prepared to admit that the relationship did become, if not sour, then at least difficult, in its final
years. The emphasis in this account is on the emotional satisfaction
of the relationship. In Moi, on the other hand, we find a far greater
emphasis on the intellectual appeal of Sartre, and the continuation
of that appeal long after the point where the couple shared common
intellectual interests. Yet what neither account can disguise is the
extent to which de Beauvoir's interest in maintaining the relationship was far greater than that of Sartre. In reading biographies of
Sartre (for example that by Annie Cohen-Solal) it is immediately
apparent that de Beauvoir does not occupy the same place in
Sartre's life as Sartre did in hers. The asymmetry of the relationship
becomes, in the accounts of Sartre, immediately apparent.

Thus in attempting to assess the relationship of de Beauvoir and
Sartre the reader plunges immediately into different interpretations
and – as Toril Moi is absolutely correct to point out – a host of her or
his own expectations, prejudices and values. It is apparently objective
to describe de Beauvoir as masochistic, because we nowadays
accept the authority of psychoanalytic interpretations of behaviour.
But it is more difficult to accept an interpretation which describes de
Beauvoir's writing as 'filled with narcissistic longings for absolute

emotional fulfilment' when so much of de Beauvoir's fiction takes as its starting point the problem of precisely that position. Over and again, de Beauvoir peoples her novels with women who have been deluded by the promise of absolute emotional fulfilment. If de Beauvoir was narcissistic it was not so much that this narcissism was expressed in the desire for absolute identity with Sartre (or A.N. Other) but in her profound belief that if she understood a position rationally and theoretically then it was removed from the realm of emotional experience and subjectivity. The narcissism in question, therefore, was a narcissism about the mind – and the degree to which mastery of the apparently abstract and theoretical world would bring with it domination. If we are to look for constant features in de Beauvoir's work (both fictional and autobiographical) we should look for the endless examples in which she cites her intelligence and her difference from other women in terms of this characteristic.

This emphasis by de Beauvoir on her difference from other women is particularly apparent in the four volumes of her auto-biography. From *Memoirs of a Dutiful Daughter* to *All Said and Done*, what de Beauvoir constantly emphasises is the degree to which in one way or another she differs from others around her. In *Memoirs* we thus have, first, de Beauvoir as the young girl who is different from others because she is far more academically gifted. Other points of separation from the world of the French bourgeoisie are also noted: de Beauvoir's family is more impoverished, and more marginal and yet more independent than all other families known to them. In the second volume, *The Prime of Life*, de Beauvoir again is different because she has achieved a recognised heterosexual relationship which is not organised in a conventional way. Again, difference is the recurring theme: different because of her interests, her profession and her travels, de Beauvoir presents herself as the first European bohemian. *Force of Circumstance* sees de Beauvoir as different in political and emotional terms from those around her: her discovery of the world outside France again carries with it a sense of her literal and metaphorical distancing from her own native culture. The return to France is the theme of *All Said and Done*; as she says in this, the final scheme of her autobiography, she finds towards the end of her life a renewed interest in her own country, from its domestic architecture to its politics.

What is remarkable about this autobiography (aside from its length, its detail and its compulsive interest) is the underlying dynamic in which de Beauvoir progresses through life by maintaining a fierce sense of her own autonomy and her separation from others. The closest relationship which therefore emerges from the autobiography is the relationship in which others are important, but only insofar as they illustrate a particular thesis or fulfil a particular need. Sartre, it is true, is always there, but he is increasingly there, after the end of the Second World War, as a generalised other, a person who represents certain political and intellectual certainties and concerns rather than a particular and specific human being. There is no doubt that de Beauvoir (as she explains in *Force of Circumstance*) is threatened by his possible loss to 'M' (Dolores Vanetti). However, this possibility occurs at the same time as de Beauvoir is involved with Nelson Algren, and one alternative reading to this crisis is that de Beauvoir was as much threatened by Algren's demands on her as she was by 'M's' demands on Sartre. The emotional dynamic, therefore, was not, essentially, one which was focused on other people, but was again about de Beauvoir's own fear of the loss of her autonomy.

Psychoanalytic theory might, and could, make short work of de Beauvoir's autobiography, since for all its protestations of objectivity and rationality it is more than possible to interpret it as a long cry of terror about the emotional encroachment of others, and particularly of conventionally masculine men. Since Sartre did not correspond to any commonplace version of masculinity, the security of his presence was always that he offered the symbolic reassurance of the masculine, but without the associations of the more ordinary attributes of masculinity. Endlessly trapped in his own version of the Peter Pan story, de Beauvoir could always play Wendy to Sartre's fantasies and needs. One of the new freedoms which readers have in the 1990s, and which de Beauvoir certainly did not have in the 1960s and 1970s when she was writing her autobiography, is to suggest that we do not have to accept individual's autobiographical accounts of themselves in either the literal or the metaphorical sense. This freedom is enormously important in the case of de Beauvoir. The new material (letters, diaries, accounts by third parties) published by and about her since her death have demonstrated that her autobiographies are partial, even by the standards of auto-biography. This much is apparent to anyone who wishes to undertake the exercise of matching de Beauvoir's text to available information. But on another level than the purely empirical, it is now permissible to interpret de Beauvoir in different ways: to read her (if we so wish) as literally true, and as a woman deeply involved in a rewarding intellectual relationship, or to read her as a woman pre-occupied with defending herself against emotional loss and determined to collude with the infantile behaviour of a man whose very infantilism towards women allowed her – as the 'different' woman – both freedom from emotional involvement and absolute emotional control.

Readers do not, of course, have to adopt either of these two somewhat extreme positions. But what it is impossible to ignore in de Beauvoir's autobiography is her narcissism, and the degree to which she is sometimes quite prepared to accept a masochistic position in order to maintain it. Thus she was endlessly prepared to sanction Sartre's relationships with other women and through this masochistic defence maintain her own position. Clearly, she did experience suffering and pain in her emotional life with Sartre. At the same time, the letters and diaries published after her death sug-gest that she was quite capable of the familiar stable mate of masochism, which is sadism. In taking on the role of critic number one of Sartre's work she placed herself in a position of absolute intellectual authority, and an authority which Sartre was clearly pre-pared for some considerable time to accept. De Beauvoir read and criticised, edited and commented upon all of Sartre's major works, and her autobiography contains numerous references to the critical and editorial work she did on Sartre's behalf. Theirs was a common intellectual project, and after Sartre's death it was the manuscript of his *Cahiers pour une morale* (posthumously published in 1983) which de Beauvoir was most concerned to retrieve from the pos-session of Arlette Elkaïm. The involvement by de Beauvoir in Sartre's writing is not, of course, in itself sadistic (and de Beauvoir was, after all, only following in the long tradition of women who have acted as secretaries and research assistants to their male com-panions), but what became possible through this close intellectual association was a degree of control over Sartre's actions and

thoughts which was *potentially* sadistic in its implications. In the
letters Sartre sent to de Beauvoir (published as the collection
Witness to My Life) there are numerous examples which suggest
that de Beauvoir was more than able to manipulate Sartre with her
comments and suggestions (Sartre, 1992b). For example, Sartre,
perhaps accurately, refers to her as 'my little judge' and in another
letter thanks her for her comments about his emotional state. Thus:

> As for my relationship with you, that's odd. Yet I tend to believe you,
> because in November you'd figured out that I was depressed long before
> I'd felt it myself. It amazes me . . . You seem to have a surer sense of one
> than I do. (1992b: 417)

The exchange of letters from Sartre to de Beauvoir ends in 1939,
and so it is impossible to see how the dynamic noticeable between
them in the 1930s progressed in the 1940s and 1950s. What we
know from de Beauvoir is that she and Sartre proceeded to spend a
great deal of time with each other, increasingly doing so as public
figures. Both produced considerable amounts of work during this
time and both became internationally famous. From de Beauvoir's
letters to Sartre (which continue up to 1963) we can detect a consistent pattern of the expression of concern alongside equivocal
remarks about others. For example, in 1955 de Beauvoir writes to
Sartre (who is on holiday with Michelle Vian) that: 'I suppose
Michelle's still driving with skill and prudence – and without any
bad luck. I've never had any doubts about Michelle, but luck's
treacherous so sometimes while dropping asleep, I've felt the odd
tremor of fear' (1991: 511). Eight years later, again when Sartre is on
holiday with a woman friend (in this case Arlette Elkaïm) de
Beauvoir writes: 'I'd really like a few words, just to reassure me
that you're alive, and that Arlette's a bit less pale than when we said
goodbye' (1991: 515).

This potent mixture of concern and negative comment *about
others* is a constant feature of de Beauvoir's letters to Sartre. In
these letters, Sartre is never criticised except for failing to write to
de Beauvoir or for theoretical misunderstandings. As such, he
remains the privileged and in a sense superhuman being of his
infancy and childhood. But because he is treated by de Beauvoir as
the child who can do no wrong (and as the child who has a right to
be entertained and properly admired by others), he remains as a

person for whom adult emotional action and choice is impossible. The women whom de Beauvoir tacitly encourages Sartre to see are as toys to a child: there to entertain and to fill the time before the child enters the adult world. The adult world in this case being the reappearance of de Beauvoir and continued engagement in public political and intellectual projects. The breakdown of this pattern occurred over the entry into Sartre's life of two individuals who refused the place assigned to them by de Beauvoir.

The two individuals who brought about this transformation were Arlette Elkaïm and Benny Lévy. Arlette first entered Sartre's life in 1956 when, according to Bair, she 'telephoned Sartre to ask him to discuss *Being and Nothingness* with her' (1990: 461). Sartre agreed to this and soon the two had embarked upon an affair. At first, de Beauvoir had little interest in Arlette or her place in Sartre's life, since she had assumed, with good reason, that Arlette would soon tire of running errands for Sartre just as Sartre would tire of her. But although this had been the pattern in previous relationships, in this case the relationship was to prove enduring. In 1965, with no reference to de Beauvoir, Sartre adopted Arlette Elkaïm as his daughter. Bair sums up the verdict of three of Sartre's biographers by quoting Ronald Hayman (1987: 404), who saw the adoption as an act of aggression against de Beauvoir; Cohen-Solal (1987: 452), in whose view the adoption was an act of faith in the future; and John Gerassi (quoted in Bair, 1990: 496), whose interpretation suggested that for Sartre the adoption was a means of securing both his future and that of Arlette. Whatever Sartre's given reasons, the adoption – which carried with it the crucial corollary that Arlette was now the heir of Sartre's estate – was one which structurally, quite apart from emotionally, marginalised de Beauvoir. Jean-Paul Sartre had now become an adult person with a daughter – a definitively family tie had been constructed which earned with it the conventional force of the priority of family over friendship.

From all the evidence which is now available to us, it would appear that Arlette Elkaïm seriously disturbed the emotional certainties of the last 18 years of de Beauvoir's life. Sartre became increasingly dependent on Arlette, and although *Adieux* gives the impression that de Beauvoir was centrally involved in the physical care of Sartre in the last years of his life, it was in fact Arlette (and other women) who did a great deal of the day-to-day care of Sartre. As de Beauvoir increasingly recognised, the function of chief carer gave Arlette considerable control over Sartre, and central importance to him. As Sartre's illness and physical decline accelerated, so the tensions between Arlette and de Beauvoir about Sartre became more explicit and more open.

In this shift in the changing patterns of relationships around Sartre, Arlette was joined by Benny Lévy. This young man had become Sartre's secretary in 1973 and was to remain so until Sartre's death. He had made Sartre's acquaintance during the *'événements'* of 1968 and attempted – finally with success – to persuade Sartre to engage in radical, left-wing politics. Lévy was at this stage in his career a convinced Maoist and would attack Sartre about the bourgeois nature of his politics and writing. These were the days of the Red Guard, the Cultural Revolution and the wholesale condemnation of bourgeois institutions and understanding. With other radical voices of the time (including Michel Foucault and Claude Mauriac) Sartre took part in denunciations of the policy of the French state in prisons and factories.

But by 1973 Sartre's physical collapse had become marked and considerable. He became virtually blind (with only a little lateral vision) and his mind slowed down to such an extent that for long periods of time he was virtually lost in torpor. It was in these years that he and de Beauvoir embarked upon the series of recorded interviews in which they questioned each other about their lives. The interviews were published in *Adieux* and provide a sometimes sentimental but often revealing account of the couple's view of each other. De Beauvoir is the more forceful questioner, with Sartre much more apparently willing to play the part of the person interviewed. In the interviews there is a great deal of repetition of previously stated positions, but occasionally an element of surprise or originality slips in. More interesting of all is the section which begins with de Beauvoir's question to Sartre, 'Let's now speak of your relationships with women, what would you say about that?' (1984: 370).

What Sartre had to say on the subject is fairly standard stuff for the author of *Words* and *The Age of Reason*. Women have always been, he says, creatures of great interest of fascination to him.

Under de Beauvoir's questioning, Sartre reveals details of his initial sexual encounter, his attitude to other women and some of his feelings about them. But his initial description of women as people to be seduced is marked in the interview, in which the person endlessly seduced is Simone de Beauvoir. Sartre does this by making a sharp distinction between pretty women, with whom he had an essentially private relationship, and de Beauvoir with whom he says he had a relationship truly *'dans le monde'*. On at least three occasions in this interview, de Beauvoir is given a special place, a public place, in Sartre's life. Whatever his physical infirmity, it is apparent that this particular man had lost none of his ability to seduce with his mind.

The intellect as an erotic zone is the impression which emerges most strongly from these interviews and from much of the auto-biographical work of both Sartre and de Beauvoir. By comparison with de Beauvoir, Sartre wrote almost nothing directly about himself except for the brief memoir of his childhood, *Words*. Yet in that short text Sartre manages to convey with extraordinary skill the nature of his relationship in the world – a relationship in which the world has to be won by words. Sartre's infancy and childhood were marked by a strong female presence and a degree of solitariness; what this rather ugly and cross-eyed little boy and adolescent was to discover was that with words he could win over women, control men and create for himself, through others, a universe in which his words were regarded as authoritative. At those points in his life when the outside world invaded Sartre's personal space (national service-conscription before and in the Second World War and imprisonment as a captured soldier) he simply created for himself an alternative world through words. His wartime diaries and his letters to de Beauvoir of the same period all attest to his ability to create for himself his own version of reality (Sartre, 1993).

Faced with this man who could literally construct for himself the world in which he wished to live (one in which he was endlessly surrounded by women and yet supported by one particular female intelligence), de Beauvoir inevitably had to play her part with words too if she wished to remain central to Sartre. It is easy to see how she became Sartre's conscience or super-ego, a role which only began to diminish as Sartre moved into a relationship with a woman

(Arlette) in which he was as much the father and the public figure as the private seducer. Thus between them de Beauvoir and Sartre created a web of words, a web as potent as anything described by Laclos and a web which has proved to be of enduring fascination to students of twentieth century intellectual history. Because, of course, part of the endless allure of Sartre and de Beauvoir is as much the relationship between them as their published works. *The Second Sex* and much of Sartre's philosophy would be major works of the twentieth century even if written by reclusive bourgeois figures. Since they were not, and since de Beauvoir in particular attempted to forge a new relationship for herself to words, the couple remain of consistent interest.

It is therefore this passionate involvement by de Beauvoir with words and language which perhaps accounts for so much of her appeal to biographers. She realised at an early stage in her life (indeed her childhood) that if she could acquire a control of language she could acquire a measure of control over an apparently hostile and unattractive social world. Having made this discovery and learned the glories of academic success, her subsequent triumphs at school and university fell easily into place. Moreover, her skill at argument and debate brought her, when only 20, a prize which she had long dreamt of, a male other who could match her skill at words and enter with her on the great adventure of the construction of a personal world. In this world the others which both parties met along the way could be translated into information or gratification or simply material. The collusive nature of the enterprise of life which de Beauvoir and Sartre shared, at least for some considerable time if not for their whole lives, is evident from the letters exchanged between them. In endless situations relationships with *others* are offered to *the other* as evidence about the nature of the world.

The part of others in the history of de Beauvoir is thus one in which those others are almost universally marginal to the central de Beauvoir/Sartre project. Nevertheless, both figures retain close relationships with their mothers; all biographers of both have noted the scrupulous attention which both paid to their mothers and the support (both material and social) which they provided for them. This support was greater in the case of Sartre, who lived with his mother for a considerable amount of his adult life, but it was still considerable in the case of de Beauvoir. She retained a close and supportive relationship with her sister until her death; after de Beauvoir's death Hélène de Beauvoir was to be a faithful advocate for her sister. Apart from these family members, both Sartre and de Beauvoir retained close relationships with the people whom they and their biographers described as 'The Family'. This group was made up of Olga Kosakievicz (of the trio and de Beauvoir's early days of teaching), Jacques Bost (a one time lover of de Beauvoir and subsequently Olga's husband), Claude Lanzmann (a lover of de Beauvoir), and Michelle Vian and Wanda Kosakievicz, women with whom Sartre had at one time been involved. Other people frequently became close to Sartre and/or de Beauvoir (as Albert Camus had been to Sartre during the Second World War or Violette Leduc was to be to de Beauvoir during the 1950s), but these relationships often ended in political disagreement (as was the case for Sartre and Camus) or a gradual loss of interest in each other (as was the case for de Beauvoir and Leduc).

In the case of de Beauvoir, Deidre Bair has documented de Beauvoir's material generosity to her friends. She would often (and this was also true of Sartre) provide individuals with money and other help. Equally, in her post-1970 'feminist period' she was to be generous with time and money to organisations and institutions. Against this material generosity, we have to set de Beauvoir's often clinical attitude to people, an attitude which can be found throughout her autobiography in her descriptions of other people. Characteristic of her attitude to others is the limited perception of the meaning of the relationship to the other person. We are told a great deal about what the particular relationship means to de Beauvoir, but we are told much less frequently about the impact of the relationship on the other. Yet the nature of that impact can be guessed only too clearly in many cases, and what emerges is a sense of the relationship as negative for the other party. In two cases in point (de Beauvoir's relationship with Olga and her relationship with Lise – both important narratives in *The Prime of Life*) what seems apparent is the absence, on de Beauvoir's part, of any understanding of the influence which she had on people younger and more impressionable than herself. When Sartre and de

Beauvoir meet Olga she is a pupil at the Lycée where de Beauvoir
taught. An able pupil, Sartre and de Beauvoir rapidly persuade Olga
that she should not study medicine (as her parents expect her to)
but should follow them to Paris and train for a career on the stage.
This training was largely to consist of long conversations with
Sartre and a few stage appearances.

De Beauvoir was later to recognise that her impact on Olga's life
was not necessarily positive and in *The Prime of Life* she was to
write:

> Instead of peaceably enjoying a normal relationship with Olga, we
> invented a myth and put it in her place. This piece of eccentricity can
> only be explained in terms of the loathing which the adult world aroused
> in us; rather than compromise with *that*, Sartre had plunged into neuro-
> sis, and I frequently told myself, weeping, that growing older meant
> falling into decay... We loaded her with values and symbols. She
> became Rimbaud, Antigone, every *enfant terrible* that ever lived, a dark
> angel judging us from her diamond-bright heaven. She did nothing to
> provoke such a metamorphosis herself; on the contrary, it irritated her,
> and she detested the fantastic character who had usurped her place.
> But she was powerless to prevent herself being absorbed. (1962a: 242)

Thus Olga is caught up in the dynamic of the lives of Sartre and de
Beauvoir. Although chronologically only separated from them by
some 10 years, she was clearly, as de Beauvoir admits above,
entirely unable to prevent herself from being usurped by the flat-
tery, the interest and the sheer seductiveness of both the adults.
Sartre in particular became obsessed with the possession of Olga;
he wished her to view him as the most important person in this
world and in order to secure this position set out to flatter her with
the full attention of his verbal powers.

Upsetting and disturbing as this attention was later to become
(and exactly how was immortalised in *She Came to Stay*), de
Beauvoir initially welcomed the existence of Olga in her life and that
of Sartre because Olga had the ability to shake Sartre out of his
depressive state. She wrote of Sartre's attentions to Olga: 'I did not
mind this; I much preferred the idea of Sartre angling for Olga's
emotional favours to his slow collapse from some hallucinatory psy-
chosis' (1962a: 241). Sartre's interest in the seduction (both
emotional and physical) of Olga thus becomes, for de Beauvoir, a
useful guarantee of Sartre's emotional stability and the first instance

in a pattern which was to be repeated throughout their lives. Sartre appears to have been endlessly prone to fits of depression and feelings of loss of touch with reality; his literary/philosophical exercises in extracting philosophy from, for example, a glass of apricot brandy were typical of a man for whom social and material reality were constructed through his engagement with language. As he was to say of himself, and to describe in his fiction, his relationship with the material world and in particular the body was more than slightly problematic. His body, and that of others, he regarded as a distinct world and one which had little impact on the world of the mind. But human beings being what they are, Sartre was forced to confront the person as a being with a physical existence; in his relationship with Olga, as with nearly all the other women with whom he was involved, he attempted to marginalise the sexual relationship in favour of what he would describe as a relationship of seduction.

All this was no doubt deeply confusing to Olga and it is apparent from her subsequent history that she was unable to regain much direction for her life after the relationship with Sartre ended. Sartre, on the other hand, and with the help and connivance of de Beauvoir, went on to endless other relationships with women, which would always be constructed as essentially private (the de Beauvoir/ Sartre relationship being public) and which – according to Sartre – would always be about his desire to win over a particular woman. In his behaviour it is all too easy to see the behaviour of a boy who grew up with complex relations to male figures; Sartre could always 'possess' his mother and never had to face the conventional constraints of the Oedipal triangle. Yet since Sartre's stepfather literally took Sartre away from his mother, when Sartre was 12, Sartre also never lived out an adolescence in which he gradually distanced himself from her. In the *Adieux* interviews, de Beauvoir questioned Sartre about his childhood and drew from him a massive and glaring contradiction. Sartre is asked by de Beauvoir about his childhood and his relationship with his stepfather. He replied:

> *Sartre*: It would take a long time to explain the nature of my relations with my stepfather.
> *de Beauvoir*: They were the relations of childhood and adolescence.
> *Sartre*: Yes. Let's not talk about it now, chiefly because it hasn't the slightest importance as far as writing is concerned . . . he knew I

> wrote, but he didn't give a damn. Furthermore, these pieces did not
> deserve that anyone should give a damn about them. But I knew my
> stepfather took no notice. So he was perpetually the person I wrote
> against. All my life. The fact of writing was against him. (quoted in
> Fullbrook and Fullbrook, 1993: 8)

In this statement we find Sartre admitting that for him the gen-
esis of his desire to write – and to write in order to control the
world around him – was the emotional 'loss' of his mother.
Throughout his adult life we therefore find Sartre busily attempting to reclaim his mother through his writing. Of course he could
not literally do this (even though Sartre's mother, Madame Mancy,
was always proud and supportive of her son) but what writing
could do was to repair the psychic blow of separation. Writing-as-
reparation is remarked upon in psychoanalysis, and Sartre offers
an excellent example of a person motivated to write precisely
because of psychic loss.

But if this is true for Sartre, it is equally true for de Beauvoir.
She remarked in *The Prime of Life* that literature is born when
'something goes amiss' and for her she faced two occasions in her
life when she was threatened with the loss of love. As a daughter,
she had to confront the inevitable fact that she could not be her
father's lover; try as the adolescent Simone did to win her father's
approval by success at school, her father only gave her the most
grudging approval and made it plain that as a sexual being she was
seriously lacking in allure. Simone had noted that her mother had
enormous physical appeal; her childhood and adolescence was
marked by the gradual recognition that she would never have such
attraction. She then found Sartre and became successful in the
conventional heterosexual mode, but almost as soon as this success was available she was again threatened with its loss through
Sartre's relationship with Olga.

Both parties in the relationship could be seen as fuelled by the
need to repair emotional damage in their lives and to make good
that damage by the externalisation which writing makes possible.
What is interesting about the way in which both went on to write is
that they did so in archetypically gendered ways: Sartre attempted
to construct an entire epistemological system in order to explain
his predicament, while de Beauvoir used her own experiences as a

basis for her novels and her non-fiction. The 'boundaries' between de Beauvoir and her writing were thus much less clearly drawn than in the case of Sartre. This can be illustrated by turning to de Beauvoir's fiction: from *She Came to Stay* (and the even earlier *When Things of the Spirit Come First*) the characters are quite explicitly drawn from real life. In the introduction to the English edition of *When Things of the Spirit Come First*, de Beauvoir notes that in previous drafts of novels she had attempted to bring ZaZa back to life and: 'In this book I kept close to reality... I drew a more faithful and a more engaging portrait of her than I had done in earlier versions' (1983: 8). In a similar pattern, Olga is to become Xavière in *She Came to Stay* and in *The Mandarins* we find scarcely disguised portraits of Algren, Sartre and Camus. The 'general' character who occurs throughout de Beauvoir is the woman who has given up all interests in life for a male lover; this woman is Paule in *The Mandarins*, Elisabeth in *She Came to Stay* and the narrator of *A Woman Destroyed*. The arguments in all these novels about the woman deluded by romance is always the same: the very idea of romantic, heterosexual, monogamous love is a trap and a delusion. Men, the argument goes, will always survive this form of relationship, but for women it is inevitably an oppressive and ultimately destructive relationship.

The passion with which this argument is made in de Beauvoir's fiction suggests the strength of de Beauvoir's fears and concerns about the subject. But what is not identified, or deconstructed, is the nature of the subject who creates these fears. Those subjects are of course men, and what is taken for granted throughout the fiction is the predatory nature of male sexuality, and its apparently natural inclination away from monogamy and towards endless sexual conquest. De Beauvoir's father is an obvious model behind this construction; as a significant other he clearly played a dominant part in the organisation of his daughter's ideas about masculinity. What de Beauvoir did with this perception was to develop a defensive strategy against the loss and threat of women which this kind of behaviour offered. To safeguard herself and other women against the negative possibilities of being emotionally consumed by male sexual adventuring, she developed a way of life and an epistemology which was located in intellectual life and individualism.

The terror of loss, and particularly the black night of the terror of the loss of male sexual love which afflicts many heterosexual women, has been a recurrent theme in Western literature for centuries. De Beauvoir was far from being the first person to address the theme; what was unusual was her creation of women characters who illustrated the theme *and* the depiction of an alternative. Having lived through the very possibility which some of her women characters were to represent, she had learned that the way to maintain the relationship which she most valued was to take on the responsibility for that potentially threatening and damaging male sexuality. Thus after the Olga incident we find de Beauvoir, committed to independence as she is, taking on the responsibility for Sartre's sexual life. She becomes the organiser, the confidante of his lovers and in all occupying the classic female space of emotional worker. When Sartre's adventures with women become too complex or when the women are upset by his behaviour, they all turn to de Beauvoir for explication and nurturance. For some 30 years de Beauvoir manages Sartre's emotional life; from a position of apparent detachment she guides him through the various complexities of his affairs and offers to him the comforting explanation that the reason why 'other' women become upset is because they have deluded beliefs about heterosexual love.

This breathtaking collusion with a particularly predatory heterosexual male would elicit comment in the behaviour of any person. For a woman, and an apparent feminist, it is particularly remarkable. Yet the evidence is unshakeable; in diaries and letters we have endless instances of de Beauvoir's grim determination to maintain a place in Sartre's life by being the figure of authority in the organisation of his sexuality. For a boy who has been brought up by a doting mother, the pattern was instantly recognisable and instantly resonant. The adored *Poulon* of his mother's life now became the equally adored Sartre for de Beauvoir. In this dynamic, de Beauvoir had once been hurt by the threat of the loss of Sartre's love, but having recovered she constructed a position for herself in which others, and not herself, became vulnerable to the loss of Sartre's affections.

As a system, this was to work reasonably well for most of Sartre and de Beauvoir's lives. It was threatened seriously by Sartre's affair with Dolores, but it is apparent from de Beauvoir's letters to Sartre in this period that she had managed to plant serious doubts in Sartre's mind about Dolores. Thus, for example she writes of Dolores to Sartre in January 1947: 'She drank one whisky after another, and this was reflected in a certain nervousness, a certain volubility, and some classic crazy behaviour' (1991: 415). And two days later:

> I really do find her extremely pleasant and likeable. Just a bit too much of a 'good lady' as Bost puts it, for my taste. But if you're male, and what is more inspired by an imperialistic passion of generosity, no more appropriate person could be met with. (1991: 419)

In these descriptions de Beauvoir has successfully given the impression of Dolores as a rather chatty conventional woman, perfectly suitable for a male sexual conquest, but not really a serious grown-up person.

In many other instances we can find examples of de Beauvoir's summaries of Sartre's women friends, summaries which effectively reduce the standing of the woman concerned and of course translate them from active participants in a relationship, with their own agendas, needs and desires, into passive recipients of Sartre's passing interest. Inevitably, the 'other' women were damaged by this attitude: Olga, as already suggested, found it difficult to regain a sense of interest and control over her life after her involvement with Sartre. Michelle Vian and Olga's sister Wanda similarly found that life with Sartre was complex. Deidre Bair has described the way in which both women turned to de Beauvoir for comfort. She writes thus of de Beauvoir's role in supporting Michelle:

> Even though they had long been used to his unorthodox behaviour and arbitrary decisions, all Sartre's other women were bewildered by what he had done in adopting Arlette. As always, it was Beauvoir who had to deal with everything, from Wanda's hysterical and destructive behaviour to a sharp acceleration in Michelle's habitual heavy drinking, now a serious problem. All during her long relationship with Sartre, Michelle had maintained a more permanent liaison with another man, but he died unexpectedly just at the time Sartre adopted Arlette. Sartre wanted to distance himself from Michelle's emotional distress, which her lover's death had exacerbated. He urged Beauvoir to take care of the sweet woman who had been so devoted to him, so Beauvoir spent long hours talking to and caring for the distraught Michelle, who needed constant

reassurance that nothing would change in her relationship with Sartre. Despite her own bouts of alcoholic crying, Beauvoir had a fastidious distaste for 'bleary-eyed drunken bleatings', but she endured them patiently for his sake and to comfort Michelle for her long years of devoted service to the Family. (Bair, 1990: 497)

De Beauvoir's support services for Sartre are made explicit in this passage. Over and again, she helped to console the women who had been upset in various ways by Sartre. Only once, in the case of Lanzmann's sister, Evelyne Ray, was de Beauvoir unable to hold and contain a woman's pain and sense of emotional loss. In conversation with Bair about Evelyne, de Beauvoir said:

She was a person of extraordinary kindness and generosity. She kept a place, a kind of shelter or aid station, for people who needed help, and she was often there sweeping and scrubbing and doing menial work. I suppose she was too intellectual to be simply an actress, but Sartre still wrote *The Condemned of Altona* for her. She didn't have the fire an actress needs to succeed, so she never got any other parts unless Sartre got them for her. Politics interested her and she wanted to take a role, but she was a woman so she could not, and of course because of Sartre and his need to keep their liaison private, she could have no role at all. I think this pained her.

Sartre was too busy, he had too many women, too many other commitments, so he could not give her too much of himself. She suffered because of that, so she began to have these liaisons. She had a lot of men, and they all adored her, but they didn't make her happy. Little by little, she couldn't stand life anymore. She was getting old [almost thirty], and she had trouble accepting the idea of aging. But it was this very, very, great, great friendship she had for Sartre that scarred her enormously. She couldn't handle it that she could not exhibit this friendship in public because he did not want her to. And she wanted children, and of course that was out of the question. So she wrote very nice little letters to everyone, to her brothers, to me, Sartre, her friends. And then she killed herself. (Bair, 1990: 462)

Yet if Sartre was able to inflict pain on women, de Beauvoir was not without the same ability – towards men – herself. The crucial case was her relationship with Nelson Algren, a relationship which certainly ended in tears, albeit of rage, on Algren's part. We do not know if Sartre used the same methods to devalue Algren as de Beauvoir had used towards Sartre's women. It seems unlikely. The disparities in the relationship – of Sartre's manifest lack of interest in de Beauvoir's lovers – suggest a complete absence of jealousy on his behalf. To Sartre, secure in the position which de Beauvoir had helped to create for him – that of the massive intellectual figure of the twentieth century – there can have been little threatening about the men with whom de Beauvoir was involved, particularly since several of them were close friends of Sartre. Extending the boundaries of 'the family' was an exercise in which Sartre and de Beauvoir engaged throughout their lives.

The glaring silence by Sartre about his life with de Beauvoir leaves any account of de Beauvoir with little to set against her version of events. What we can note about the pair, however, is that in both cases there was often little engagement with other intellectual figures. It is obviously not the case that Sartre was not involved in intellectual life, but much more that for a considerable part of his later life he was isolated from developments in European intellectual debates. The Communist Party and Marxism were presences in Sartre's life throughout the 1940s and 1950s, but after this point Sartre found himself increasingly isolated from the shifts (towards psychoanalysis, structuralism and deconstruction) which were to form key themes of the 1970s and 1980s. As the intellectual map of France became dominated by figures such as Lacan, Derrida and Foucault, Sartre's liberal humanism was increasingly seen as out-of-date. Sartre's frantic attempts to involve himself in radical politics via Maoism sat uneasily with the work of a man whose interests had always been based in high bourgeois European culture.

So history, or intellectual history, passed Sartre by. As he became marginalised, so de Beauvoir was discovered and rediscovered. We can look in vain in her memoirs for mention of engagement with feminism prior to about 1970; after that point her life and interests are transformed by it and she becomes part of a global movement. Thus she is rescued from isolation by events, just as Sartre is forced into greater isolation by the changing nature of intellectual life. But in an important sense isolation was no new experience to either of them, and a final remark about 'others' in the lives of both, and particularly de Beauvoir, was that her life always had an isolated quality to it – an isolated quality created in part by the sense of Sartre-as-the-world. In *Memoirs of a Dutiful Daughter* de Beauvoir recalls how, as a child, she used to hide under her father's desk. The story, in the light of subsequent events and subsequent readings of de Beauvoir, has a wonderful metaphorical strength to it. Here is the little girl, later the woman, hiding under that symbol of masculine intellectual engagement, the sacred desk in the paternal study. It is a story which in a sense says a great deal about de Beauvoir and her place in the intellectual world for much of her life.

But what happened to de Beauvoir is that European intellectual life started to deconstruct, metaphorically, the father's desk. It did so through feminism, psychoanalysis, deconstructionism and all the other radical intellectual shifts of intellectual engagement in the 1970s and the 1980s. And as this occurred, what was found so to speak under the desk was de Beauvoir – a woman who had grown up in the shadow of high bourgeois European patriarchal culture and yet had offered an alternative reading of the part of women in that culture. To have done so in 1949, at a time when the Cold War was just beginning to lay the ideological foundations of the sexually conservative 1950s was then seen as nothing short of outstanding. Women reading de Beauvoir in the 1960s and 1970s frequently noted their amazement at the date of publication of the book, and (though less frequently) an equal amazement at both its success and its isolation. Again, the theme of de Beauvoir-as-different emerges. Western feminism in the 1960s and 1970s placed its major emphasis on the similarities between women *as* women. 'Sisterhood is powerful' and 'universal Sisterhood' were slogans of the women's movement and as such they asserted both the intrinsic strengths of women and the intrinsic difference between women and men. That women were emphatically different from men, had different concerns and different interests, were general and shared assumptions.

This new political culture of feminism then turned to find a common past, and of course in doing so found de Beauvoir. The paradox of this discovery was that *The Second Sex* was difficult to integrate into second wave feminism since its conclusions suggested that women should be more like men. De Beauvoir's conclusions all pointed to the need for greater female autonomy, and her subsequent engagement with feminism was entirely consistent with this view. Thus in the 1970s she became involved in campaigns for abortion rights in France and also for improved state provision for abused women and women in employment. All these aims and programmes would be shared by the majority of feminists in any culture, but what was so striking about de Beauvoir's involvement in feminism was her refusal to countenance the discussions of the more complex issues raised by feminists concerning language and sexuality. Indeed, since France was the European country par excellence in which questions about gender and language were raised (in the work of Cixous, Irigaray and Kristeva) it is all the more remarkable that for de Beauvoir, language, like the body, remained sealed and final. Language, she maintained, could not be gendered; only *what* was said could be seen in female or male terms. Equally, while de Beauvoir obviously endorsed the liberal feminist position on rights and recognition for bisexual or lesbian women, she was always at pains to assert her own heterosexuality and the absolutely asexual nature of her relationship with Sylvie le Bon. To protest too much we have come to see as suspicious in itself, and certainly the comments by de Beauvoir about this relationship all reinforce the theme discussed earlier in this chapter about de Beauvoir's fear of the erosion of emotional boundaries, or any attack on her own autonomy. As fulsome as de Beauvoir is in *All Said and Done* about Sylvie and contemporary feminism, it is difficult not to read the account as one written by someone for whom the problems of womanhood are problems of the others.

6

Reading de Beauvoir

When Simone de Beauvoir died in 1986 she was hailed as the greatest feminist of the twentieth century, if not ever. One of the speakers at the funeral, the French feminist Elisabeth Badinter, declared 'women, you owe everything to her' (quoted in Bair, 1990: 617). Deidre Bair concludes her biography of de Beauvoir by remarking 'she may have been a mass of contradictions, but she was still, in the most profoundly respectful sense of the phrase, "the mother of us all"' (1990: 618). These opinions were voiced before the publication of the letters between Sartre and de Beauvoir and the revelations about their dealings with others. Equally, it is clear from reading biographies of other leading figures of postwar French intellectual life that not everyone shared such a positive view of de Beauvoir or Sartre. For example, in his biography of Michel Foucault, David Macey makes it clear that Foucault had little time for the ideas of Sartre and de Beauvoir, and although he was prepared to afford Sartre grudging respect he had no toleration for de Beauvoir, indeed she was capable of reducing him to apoplectic rage (Macey, 1994: 429).

From biographies such as Macey's there emerges a picture of French intellectual life which is not to be found in de Beauvoir, nor in accounts of her life. Indeed, one of the features of de Beauvoir's autobiography is the sense which she communicates of a small intellectual community, and a limited social world. The main figures of her life, 'the family' as they are referred to in her autobiography, largely constitute the world in which she lives, and the appearance of other figures of academic and intellectual life is limited. De Beauvoir certainly mentions (and who could not?) her meetings with Castro, Picasso, Giacometti and other giants of the twentieth century, but there is relatively little discussion of other figures who made up more local communities. In part, of course, this absence of other associations and networks lay in de Beauvoir's existence as a writer. From the end of the Second World War she lived independently of professional structures and networks, and the one public initiative in which she was involved *(Les Temps Modernes)* was very much part of her personal life.

Thus, for a major intellectual figure, de Beauvoir lived in many ways an exclusive and a very private life. It would not be entirely accurate to describe this as 'isolated' since she lived a life which bound her into intimate relationships with a number of people, but her life nevertheless had a quality of isolation about it, in which she created for herself (and Sartre) an enclosed world, both socially and theoretically, from which they seldom had reason to move. We can look in vain in de Beauvoir's work for a discussion, and in particular a discussion of the relevance for her, of the innovations in European thought occasioned by Lacan, or Irigaray, or Foucault or any of the other writers on literature and psychoanalysis who contributed so centrally to European intellectual life in the 1960s and 1970s. These names and these currents are simply absent or if present only mentioned in passing when mention is unavoidable. It would be an exaggeration to say that de Beauvoir's world was hermetically sealed, but it would be appropriate to suggest that having created in the late 1940s a clear view of the world, she then remained entirely faithful to it.

When de Beauvoir was 'discovered' by feminism in the late 1960s – and annexed for feminism – her view of the world gave rise to numerous problems about how this woman could be described as a feminist and how her work could be used to demonstrate a theoretical tradition in feminism. In the late 1960s and early 1970s Western feminism needed to discover, to claim, a past. It could do this by historical research and the rediscovery of the lives of previously silent women. In this writers such as Sheila Rowbotham (1973) were enormously significant in pointing to the past, and 'history' as its theoretical construction, and demanding that 'history' be asked some different questions. Equally, and particularly in the United States, women of colour began to speak with a new voice of their silence and of the experiences of the previously silenced. Both developments spoke of, and spoke to, the absence from Western high culture of accounts of the experiences of poor and dispossessed women. Just as male socialist historians reclaimed the past of the male working class, so women historians and writers claimed and voiced the experiences of the vast majority of Western women who had previously had no access to recording their own lives.

De Beauvoir clearly lay somewhat apart from this tradition. Her intellectual career had all been about European high culture and one of the most abstract and bourgeois of its forms – namely philosophy. At no point in de Beauvoir's writing did she engage with what might be described as working class culture; *The Second Sex* has passing references to 'the milliner's apprentice, the shop-girl and the secretary', but the essential engagement of the book is with an intellectual and artistic élite. De Beauvoir asks rhetorically 'How could Van Gogh have been born a woman?' and her answer is, inevitably, that Van Gogh only became a great painter because he was able to live the kind of life which was acceptable for men. Women, de Beauvoir argues, could not have travelled or frequented cafés in the same way as he did, and because of this were unable to produce art with any great qualities of experience and variety. Running rapidly through two dozen or so figures of the European gallery of great literary and artistic achievement, de Beauvoir finds no women to set alongside Tolstoy and Dostoyevsky. The great women writers she finds limited by their range of experience and their partial engagement with the culture.

All this, of course, suggests a more than slightly élitist view of the world. We could add up the 'great' artists of the world, and find more men than women, but equally we might observe that in every generation of men there are relatively few who achieve lasting eminence of any kind. Very few people in the late twentieth century would bother to deny that women's absence from the cultural hall of fame is due to structural reasons as much as any other. We can all agree with de Beauvoir when she argues that women's domestic responsibilities make it more difficult for women than men to devote themselves to non-domestic activities of any kind. But we might also add that what becomes 'great' is a problematic exercise; since 1949 we have become more careful about assuming that the dead white men, whom de Beauvoir cites so approvingly, are actually the be-all and end-all of the culture.

We can defend de Beauvoir's admiration for the outstanding male figures of the Western academy by pointing out that when she was writing, at least in the period up to the mid-1960s, there was no visible feminist tradition for her to refer to. Her education was by men and about men. Women simply did not appear in her world except as her friends or the lovers of Sartre. If we accept this argument, then it leaves de Beauvoir in the position of having helped to create a feminist tradition and we do not have to ask further questions about the presences of other women whom de Beauvoir chose to ignore. Yet in the 1990s it is difficult simply to excuse de Beauvoir's masculinist bias on the grounds of female absence, if only because one of the results of contemporary feminism is that women have started to research their collective past and discovered the presence of women even in those circumstances where it had previously been supposed that none existed or was influential. The pages of the journal *Signs*, for example, are replete with carefully researched articles which demonstrate the presence, and frequently the influential presence, of women in diverse and often obscure situations. Since Paris in the latter half of the twentieth century is scarcely obscure, it has been relatively easy for women historians to demonstrate that at the same time as de Beauvoir was writing that she knew very few women, there were active and vocal groups of women pursuing feminist, or quasi-feminist, ideas as well as women artists whose work was nationally discussed. One example of the latter is Germaine Richier, whose sculpture was a matter of general discussion in artistic circles at precisely the same time as de Beauvoir was meeting Giacometti and writing *The Second Sex*. Indeed, as the art critic Sarah Wilson has written:

> Richier frequented the cafés of Montparnasse in the company of figures such as Colette, Nathalie Sarraute and other figures around the prestigious *Nouvelle Revue Française* group, such as Dominique Aury. While

Aury, in her picaresque, neo-Sadian novel *Story of O* buried her identity
and paradoxically her sex with the pseudonym Pauline Réage (linked
instantly to her companion Paulhan), complicitly adopting Sadean
stereotypes, Richier's sexuality in conjunction with her work challenged
and disturbed conventional notions. (1993: 41)

We can turn to *The Prime of Life* and search in vain for the name
of Germaine Richier or indeed any lengthy account of the work of
Nathalie Sarraute or Dominique Aury. Yet all three were producing
work, in one form or another, at exactly the same time as de
Beauvoir and in exactly the same *milieu*. The 'cafés of
Montparnasse' only amounted to about half a dozen in terms of
those frequented by bohemian intellectuals in Paris, and thus it is
impossible that de Beauvoir did not at some point in her career
come across other women whose work was, as much as hers,
involved in the deconstruction, or at least the examination, of traditional categories of gender. Unless, of course, another dynamic
was at work: that de Beauvoir simply turned her back on other
women and on other issues which she did not choose to confront.
This possibility is particularly vivid in the case of her attitude to the
sculpture of Giacometti and Richier. Giacometti is mentioned in
The Prime of Life; Richier is not. Equally, what is not mentioned
about either of them is the way in which both dehumanise the
human form and to a certain extent attempt to represent the
human body in androgynous terms. It is interesting that de
Beauvoir suggests, in the review of great dead men which concludes *The Second Sex*, that even allowing for the achievements of
men in the past, 'Today the expressive arts are not the only ones
open to women; many are essaying various creative activities'
(1964b: 662). There, on her doorstep in Paris, was a woman doing
precisely that, and yet not used as an example to illustrate de
Beauvoir's point. Richier's work qualifies her for a place on de
Beauvoir's list of successful women, so too did her relationship
with Paulhan, a man who is mentioned frequently in *The Prime of
Life* and *Force of Circumstance*, not least because he did a great deal
to make possible the initial publication of *Les Temps Modernes*.

The example of Germaine Richier serves, therefore, to illustrate a certain pattern in de Beauvoir's view of the world: that she
could *see* men and their activities but had rather less ability to

perceive and record the actions of women. This pattern has to be qualified in two ways; first, de Beauvoir was very well aware of her women 'family' friends and of her mother and sister. Second, the selective vision about women and men disappeared, or shifted, in the late 1960s as women as a group 'discovered' de Beauvoir. The feminist search for a feminist past made it inevitable that even if de Beauvoir did not choose to notice women (or was at least selective in her perception of them) then women would notice her. Moreover, the feminism of the 1960s made the world a safer place in which to be a feminist; it is clear from her own reaction to the comments made at the time of the publication of *The Second Sex* that de Beauvoir did not enjoy or relish being described as frigid or man-hating. Her response, recorded in *Force of Circumstance*, was largely defensive – to assert that she was emphatically *not* these things, rather than discussing the judgements implicit in the accusations.

But being able to challenge misogynist and sexist attitudes only became possible long after 1949. De Beauvoir, like everyone else in the West, had to live in a moral climate in the 1950s which was deeply conservative and in many ways socially reactionary. The bleakness of the world in which many women grew up and the problems implicit in the cultural climate of the 1950s about the resolution and construction of femininity were vividly captured by Sylvia Plath in *The Bell Jar* (1966). If *Memoirs of a Dutiful Daughter* told a dismal tale of sexual repression and hypocrisy in France of the 1920s, then *The Bell Jar* was no less scathing about the Eisenhower years in the United States. De Beauvoir's world in the 1950s remained very much the world which she had always known, that of bohemian Paris and its friendship networks. What she did in these years, which mark her out from many of her contemporaries, was to become a public person and engage in radical political action.

The 'political' de Beauvoir who emerged in the 1950s was a woman who to a certain extent was following her existing political sympathies. De Beauvoir had never made any secret of her anti-bourgeois, left-wing views and with Sartre had always found common cause with other groups of the non-Communist French left. Given that the Communist Party was the largest and most organised left-wing party in France, relationships with it on the part of both de Beauvoir and Sartre were always crucial. Sartre and de Beauvoir never joined the Party, and were always true to their anarchic sympathies, but the issue of whether or not to join remains a recurrent issue throughout *Force of Circumstance*. What they both did, and very much as a couple, was to associate them-selves with particular left-wing radical causes and to lend their considerable reputations to the public support of these causes. The two issues which dominated their lives in the 1950s and the 1960s were French policy in Algeria and the war between the United States and North Vietnam. Both these issues constitute a considerable part of the narrative of *Force of Circumstance* and mark the break between de Beauvoir as a private individual and de Beauvoir as a public, global figure.

As de Beauvoir entered the public world through the publication of *The Second Sex* and her political involvements, so the accounts of her life which she provided change. *Memoirs of a Dutiful Daughter* and *The Prime of Life* are essentially about a girl and a woman liv-ing a 'private' life, but determinedly making statements about the public world and attempting to theorise human relations within it. *Force of Circumstance* and *All Said and Done* are very much about a publicly known woman, whose life is recorded in the interna-tional media and increasingly the subject of comment and evaluation. Inevitably, much of the sense of a particular world which enriches the first two volumes of the autobiography disap-pears, and we are left with comments about a world which has been widely scrutinised and examined by hundreds of writers other than de Beauvoir.

Thus the issue of the public and the private, and 'reading' the public and the private, comes to the fore in our reading and under-standing of de Beauvoir. Prior to her death and the publication of further material by and about her, it was relatively easy to 'read' de Beauvoir as an inspiring tale of female emancipation and liberation. Clearly, this was very much how de Beauvoir wished us to see her life, and readers were positively encouraged to follow this reading by the material and structure of de Beauvoir's autobiography. Both *Memoirs of a Dutiful Daughter* and *Prime of Life* end on a note of lib-eration; in the first volume, de Beauvoir is 'freed' from her family by her success in higher education and her meeting with Sartre. In the second, de Beauvoir, as a French woman, is literally freed by the end of the Second World War and the liberation of Paris in 1944. *Force of Circumstance* and *All Said and Done* end on more ambiguous notes: the conclusion to *Force of Circumstance* suggests reservations about the experiences of her life, while *All Said and Done* is very markedly about the death of God. In all, therefore, we have a life presented by its author as an exercise in personal emancipation, but an exercise which has left unresolved certain questions about existence.

Nevertheless, what comes across from the four volumes is a high degree of authorial coherence and control. The dominant tone of the autobiography is that of a woman with a clear sense of purpose. It is not that de Beauvoir minimises the emotional difficulties and problems which she encountered – on the contrary these are very explicitly spelt out. But what she does do is place these difficulties within a trajectory of control, so that in the jealousies and pains of, for example, her relationship with Nelson Algren or that of Sartre with Dolores, the reader is given a sense of a person who can resolve and understand these problems. What is seldom examined is how the problems arise, and it is only very late in her life that de Beauvoir began to ask critical questions of Sartre about his relations with women.

In her autobiographical project, de Beauvoir thus provides a rich basis for the conclusion that she is a woman making her own world: at first she did this in relationship to her personal circumstances by achieving economic independence and then she attempted to do it by intervening in the public world and placing her own views about the world on the political agenda. As she entered the second, public, stage of her life, so she became, in a sense, more private and more inclined to make distinctions, in an entirely bourgeois way, between the public and the private world. The crucial example of this is the compartmentalisation of her account of her mother's death into a separate volume of autobiography. *A Very Easy Death* is the briefest of de Beauvoir's autobiographical works (although considered by many to be the most vivid) and it is also essentially contained. What it does is to suggest to the reader an organising world view which placed the death of a mother (*the* mother in this case) in a special, separate category. In one sense, of course, this account makes sense of what is often regarded as a crucial event in anybody's life; in this case what is striking is that the death of the mother is separate, is distinct from the main current and narrative of autobiography. An alternative interpretation is that de Beauvoir saw her mother's death as so special that it deserved a special place in her work; alongside this we have to set our knowledge (and knowledge given to us by de Beauvoir herself) of her mother as a figure of crucial importance in her life.

Thus what could be read as the marginalisation of the mother could also be seen as part of a pattern in de Beauvoir which is now familiar to critics of Western culture; namely, that women are marginalised, kept separate from public life and given a status of necessary, but unfortunate. For example, in *A Very Easy Death* one of the themes which engages de Beauvoir's attention is that of why, given the very different politics of herself and her mother, she felt so strongly about her death. Here, very explicitly, is a rationalist plea about emotional life; de Beauvoir protests against that order of things which makes us love and value those with whom we do not agree. The order of things which she wished to achieve was one in which 'private' love and 'public' understanding were one. That order was, of course, precisely her view of her relationship with Sartre – that she loved him as a private person because they shared the same public views. What was absolutely not admissible to this version of events was the possibility that public agreement became essential in the absence of private affection; as Sartre increasingly became 'the public' for de Beauvoir so the relationship increasingly lost intimacy. Since de Beauvoir could see this, even if she could not admit it, she began to defend her now absent private space with particular vehemence as Sartre became involved in relationships with others.

The vacillations, the upheavals and the complexities of the Sartre/de Beauvoir relationship have now become part of the folklore and history of twentieth century intellectual life. The dominant reading of the relationship by feminists has remained, from the late 1960s onwards, one which accepts de Beauvoir's version of events: that the relationship was essentially positive and chosen. This reading fits in with a tradition of writing about de Beauvoir which runs from Carol Ascher's 1981 study *Simone de Beauvoir: A Life of Freedom* to Toril Moi's account of de Beauvoir, *Simone de Beauvoir: The Making of an Intellectual Woman*, which was published in 1994. Both authors, widely separated in terms of style and method, assert a view of de Beauvoir which essentially endorses her own, namely that she chose 'freedom' as a young girl and chose intellectual life as the means through which to pursue it. Moreover, both assent to the de Beauvoir-as-model interpretation which forms a very central core to writing, particularly in North America, about de Beauvoir. There, and most specifically in the United States, the dominant view of de Beauvoir, to judge from recent collections in feminist journals, is that of a woman who gave women a blueprint both for individual lives and the understanding of social existence. The crucial text is *The Second Sex*, and critical to it is de Beauvoir's claim that women are perceived as 'the other' and outside culture.

That understanding has now become a familiar part of conventional readings of the world. It is widely accepted that societies throughout the world distinguish nature from culture and identify women with the former and men with the latter. It is equally generally conceded that the public world of most societies, whether political or symbolic, is dominated by men. What is not so simply agreed, if agreed at all, is how the categories of 'nature' and 'culture', or 'public' and 'private' are constructed and how these categories have reflected male interests rather than absolute certainties in all societies. De Beauvoir's perception of public and private, and nature and culture, follows a traditional model which assumes these categories to be fixed and does not question the way in which these ideas have been articulated – and who has been able to articulate them. For example, when she writes about 'private', domestic life, she assumes the home as a trap for women and one from which men naturally escape. Her childhood vision of her mother at home and her father as absent-from-home informs her judgements about the construction of the private world and its material reality. What de Beauvoir rightly emphasises, therefore, is the seclusion and isolation which the home can form for women. But what she explores less is the emotional life constructed in the home, the emotional life which is not only formed by the home but by a set of relationships in which women become the keepers of the hearth through a complex series of moral and emotional nego-tiations. Françoise de Beauvoir was thus trapped in the marital home not because such was the fate of all women but because poverty and lack of education made her a helpless protagonist in conflict with her husband. More or less just across the street from Françoise de Beauvoir, Elisabeth Le Coin's mother conducted her home as a power base. She may well have spent a considerable amount of time in that home, but she did so in much the same way as a general will inhabit his headquarters.

This example serves to illustrate the singular vision that runs through de Beauvoir's life and work. It was through this singular vision, of course, that she forged the life which she aspired to and that single-mindedness of purpose shines through every page of autobiography, and every letter written. But however much we might admire this determination, other questions occur when de Beauvoir's life is assessed or used as a model for other lives and other societies. Claims by feminists that de Beauvoir is the found-ing mother of feminism raise questions about feminism, just as assertions, like Toril Moi's, that de Beauvoir is 'an intellectual woman' lead us to ask exactly what (and indeed who) intellectual women are, and what non-intellectual women are like. All these issues have become more pressing and problematic since de Beauvoir's death let loose the publication of material about her (and by her) which does not always present her in the best of lights.

Yet in saying this, moral issues are raised about how we evaluate women, and how we should assess the work of women. About de Beauvoir, it is unarguable that she fought battles (mostly with her parents) about personal liberation and claimed an emancipation for herself which was unknown to most of her contemporaries. Equally, we can qualify this by pointing out that the élitism of French higher education was such that once de Beauvoir was suc-cessful in it, the system became virtually gender blinkered about her sex. When de Beauvoir wrote in the concluding pages to *The Prime of Life* that she felt she had faced little discrimination in her career (both as a writer and a teacher) then she may well have been falsely conscious, but she may have also been right in that her academic achievements compensated for her unequal status as a woman. But in that model of achievement in an *apparently* gender blinkered system lies a crucial problem about de Beauvoir, and one which dogged her in the days of her discovery by feminism. The problem was that de Beauvoir largely perceived the system of knowledge in which she had been such a triumphant pupil as universal and far removed from material or epistemological differences of gender. Given that her subject was philosophy this perception was understandable; its very abstraction makes it difficult to relate to human differences of any kind and not just those of gender. Moreover de Beauvoir trained in European philosophy in which the human subject was never seen in those somewhat qualified, and relative terms of English empiricism. Small wonder that de Beauvoir did not make the leap from the human subject to the female/male subject for some considerable time.

When she did in *The Second Sex* and to a certain, limited extent in *Pyrrhus and Cinéas* (1944), she produced a version of the single human subject model which was as rigid in many ways as the model in which she had been educated. In a famous, and telling, remark Audré Lorde pointed out that 'the master's tools will never demolish the master's house' and those words convey precisely some of the equivocations possible about de Beauvoir (Lorde, 1984: 110–13). These equivocations might be categorised into two groups: those which relate to de Beauvoir as a role model and those which relate to de Beauvoir's understanding and analysis of the social world. The first group of problems were elegantly summed up by Margaret Walters in her comments on *The Second Sex*:

> For de Beauvoir's definition of what it means to be human – indeed her whole existential philosophy – is loaded with unacknowledged class and intellectual assumptions. This emerges most clearly when she moves from the general to the particular, and outlines the possibilities open to individual women today. (She admits, of course, that no individual can solve the problem alone, and that women will never be free without a radical transformation of society.)
>
> The emancipated woman wants to be active, a taker, and refuses the passivity man means to impose on her. The 'modern' woman accepts masculine values; she prides herself on thinking, taking action, working, creating on the same terms as man.

It is surely a bleak prospect. The emancipated woman sounds just like that familiar nineteenth-century character, the self-made man. And isn't that the model underlying all her philosophic sophistication? Early capitalist man, dominating and exploiting the natural world, living to produce, viewing his own life as a product shaped by will, and suppressing those elements in himself – irrationality, sexuality – that might reduce his moral and economic efficiency. His moral and emotional life is seen in capitalist terms – as de Beauvoir tends to see hers. She sees childhood as an apprenticeship, a time for amassing, acquiring, accumulating knowledge. Experience is often a matter of debts or credits – the image of the balance sheet recurs in her work. And the French title of her latest autobiography is *Tout compte fait* (not quite the same as the English translation, *All Said and Done*). (1976: 357)

This is fairly damning stuff. Here is the 'mother' of feminism portrayed as nothing less than a female version of male entrepreneurial capitalism, a person set on the domination of the social and political world and ruthlessly suppressing in herself feelings of vulnerability and interdependence. This person is the master, using the master's tools and set on subduing the world to his advantage. Such people are very obviously precisely those whom de Beauvoir was to attack during debates on French policy in Algeria.

In terms of what many feminists (and indeed people) now value as desirable human achievements and characteristics, the de Beauvoir of this reading does not seem an attractive person. Her will-to-power is transparent, and if she cannot personally achieve power then she sets about encouraging power-in-others. The other in her case was always Sartre; a reading of their life together could be that de Beauvoir did her utmost to make him powerful and intellectually dominant. When other people seemed to threaten this power (first other intellectuals and later in Sartre's life young secretaries) then de Beauvoir reacted with fierce defensiveness. Ensuring phallic authority thus becomes a major theme in de Beauvoir's life, and one somewhat at variance with conventional feminist readings of it. The argument against this – that de Beauvoir did much to destabilise conventional constructions of gender and with them the authority of men – is convincing about de Beauvoir's attack on the construction of traditional versions of femininity. Sonia Kruks, Judith Butler and Linda Zerilli are among those who have argued that de Beauvoir did this; to quote Linda Zerilli, '*The Second Sex*, then, provides a discursive space in which to articulate the remarkable variability of what goes under the name of the maternal experience' (1992: 123). She goes on:

> By debunking this myth, Beauvoir helped to establish, even if she did not articulate, an imaginative space for those contemporary feminists who wish to rethink the maternal. Beauvoir's concern, however, is not to suggest an alternative meaning for maternity but to expose what is at stake for the patriarchal order in the monolithic representation of the mother. (1992: 124)

Few feminists would argue that, at least in Western societies with a Judeo-Christian tradition, there has been, particularly visually, a glorification of motherhood and especially that of the relationship between mothers and sons. But at the same time, that very tradition has emphasised the negative aspects of motherhood; 'In sorrow shalt thou bring forth children', stands not as a comment about motherhood but an account of human history. De Beauvoir only had to turn to European literature to find countless examples of both women and men expressing deep reservations about maternity and about what she was to call 'forced maternity'. The point, therefore, is that we could contest de Beauvoir's reading of maternity. Equally, we could hypothesise that her initial construction of maternity – and her refusal of it in both a personal and a social sense – was one constructed out of her own feelings of having disappointed her parents in not being a boy and thus allowing them the immense social and symbolic achievement of perfectly realised motherhood. 'If only Simone had been a boy' is a remark which de Beauvoir recalls about herself in *Memoirs of a Dutiful Daughter* (1959: 177). Indeed, if she had been, as Sartre was, then her entry into part of the symbolic order of the West would have been more complete.

But if women *qua* women cannot enter the lofty temples of complete symbolic power, then at least they can, occasionally, attempt to enter the intellectual and institutional structures of male power. De Beauvoir had little time for the latter, and was never a careerist in professional terms. Her ambitions were more global and like many male intellectuals what she wished to do was to construct a coherent system of thought which could be all encompassing in its explanatory strength. For her, existentialism was this system. Her part in its construction remains disputed, with Michèle le Doeuff and Kate Fullbrook and Edward Fullbrook suggesting a much larger contribution by de Beauvoir to its form and content than previously supposed. As all these writers point out, it was de Beauvoir's *own* internalisation of conventional sexism that made it impossible for her to perceive the originality and importance of her own interventions. Consistently claiming that Sartre was the more original thinker, she refused to allow what subsequent biographical studies have demonstrated: that she saw the essential philosophical problems which Sartre was later to codify.

What this evidence does is to suggest two things: first, that de Beauvoir, in an entirely orthodox way for many women, underestimated her achievements, and – more telling in epistemological terms – refused ideas and information drawn from everyday experience. The second problem is more complex, but it is that in her attitude to knowledge de Beauvoir, far from being a good model for women (or anybody else) is actually a bad one, in that she refuses to allow unconventional constructions or interventions and that she has a deep and damaging respect for male intellectual authority. What she also had was a manifest inability and refusal to name emotional pain when its source was Sartre. As Toril Moi (1994) argues de Beauvoir's writing fluctuates between the positively vital and the positively flat – the difference being closely related to the state of her relationship with Sartre. Moi writes:

> In her published memoirs, such 'writing of disavowal' is particularly noticeable in *All Said and Done*. Written specifically to counter the impression of melancholia left by *Force of Circumstance*, the introduction to the fourth volume of her autobiography seeks not only to present her life as a success story – which of course it was – but specifically to deny the existence, in that story, of loneliness and anxiety. So much disavowal turns the volume into a lifeless ghost of an autobiography, a mere chronicle of official duties, rather than an exploration of lived experience. The same is true for *Adieux: A Farewell to Sartre*, where Beauvoir's bleak and devitalized prose conveys not only her inability to lift herself out of her sorrow, but also her resolute determination not to mention her conflicts with Sartre. For it is not only Sartre's death that pains Beauvoir, it is also his lack of loyalty to her during their final years, his betrayal of what she took to be their common ideals, and his cavalier disregard for her feelings in his dealings with other women.

> The price she pays is an almost complete blockage of affect in her lan-
> guage: on the pages of *Adieux*, her prose is dry as dust. The contrast to
> *A Very Easy Death* could not be greater: when Beauvoir finally forces
> herself to confront her long-buried feelings for her mother, she pro-
> duces the most vibrant, energetic and moving prose she ever wrote.
> (1994: 251)

This passage very effectively records the pain which de Beauvoir
bore throughout the relationship with Sartre; the reward and
solace which Sartre held out to her was that he would always
respect her intelligence and rate that quality in her above that of his
other women friends.

Yet this very reward was deeply, and for de Beauvoir painfully,
double-edged. As long as de Beauvoir was the 'witness' to Sartre's
life, the intellectual *alter ego*, the rational woman and the collusive
partner in his affairs with others, de Beauvoir was denied other
forms of agency within Sartre's life, particularly a right to her own
feelings about Sartre. Even more damaging, the emphasis on de
Beauvoir's intellectual competence (which both constructed) was
a way of separating de Beauvoir from other women. As a strategy
for maintaining de Beauvoir's place in Sartre's life this was successful for some time, but only at the cost of separating de
Beauvoir from other women and, more crucially for her own psychic state, from herself. Thus we confront the paradox of the
so-called 'mother of feminism' deliberately setting herself apart
from other women, and other forms of knowledge, in order to
maintain her position as first wife to a deeply polygamous man.

The depression and the self-doubt which inevitably ensued from
de Beauvoir's systematic alliance with the cause of formally constructed male intellectual competence have now been discussed by
various feminists. However, it is also possible to raise issues about
the relationship of women to 'knowledge' and about the definition
of feminism itself. When Toril Moi writes of 'Simone de Beauvoir:
the making of an intellectual woman' or Carol Ascher 'Simone de
Beauvoir: a life of freedom', they implicitly accept conventional definitions of 'intellectual' and 'freedom'. Readers are left to ask how
an 'intellectual' woman is different from others, and whether or not
the inevitable élitism of the term is actually appropriate as a form of
praise. It is not that de Beauvoir was not an intellectual, she clearly

was. It is rather more that the term carries with it, as does 'freedom', questions about our culture's need to label certain forms of
thought as different and more 'intellectual' than others. De
Beauvoir herself (as suggested above) long did this, and endlessly
refused the worth of some of her insights and ideas because they
were insufficiently systematised in conventional ways. The problem for feminists writing about de Beauvoir then becomes one of
mining the rich seam of her work for the golden nuggets of insight
and perception buried in a great deal of fairly dull earth. For
example, one can only hope that de Beauvoir's travels were more
interesting to her than to her reader; *America Day by Day* (1952)
and *The Long March* (1958) are particularly vivid examples of the
way in which de Beauvoir (and indeed the intellectualising impulse)
can make the world deeply boring by the need to theorise. When
she writes about the ugly clothes sold to the mass market in New
York, she conveys exactly that sense of pointless repetition which
anyone who has shopped in any chain store has experienced.
Unfortunately, she then has to organise the reader's reaction by
comments about freedom and true conditions of freedom.

In making de Beauvoir, or any other woman, a feminist icon,
there are always dangers of refusing the problems which her life
raises. De Beauvoir herself repeatedly refused to acknowledge certain forms of emotional pain; we can now detect her sense of her
inappropriate sex and her struggle to find a source of alliance
through which to maintain her relationship with Sartre. But in
acknowledging them we also have to ask about the source of these
problems; it is now insufficient, and indeed damaging, to use de
Beauvoir as an example to women, since in so many ways the paths
which she followed were fraught with destructive possibilities.
Much of the vitality of her work comes from her wish to create a
secure world for herself, a world in which she will be acknowledged by Sartre and free from fears about feminine inadequacy. As
readers we are the happy heirs to this insecurity. But as readers
and writers who might wish to pass on an understanding of relations between the sexes, there is also a responsibility to make
apparent the processes through which de Beauvoir emerged as a
writer. She was uniquely fortunate in being able to turn her inse-
curities to advantage. Her education and social background helped

to make this possible and to give her an initial sense of being both competent and different from other women. Yet for all that, she was a woman and as such subject to the same pressures as other women. That sense of similarity, of sameness, of shared experience, was never to emerge in her written work. It is thus the task of the reader (in whom de Beauvoir generally has little trust) to raise those issues in de Beauvoir's work which she so manifestly wished to ignore.

Bibliography

Works by Simone de Beauvoir

Cited in order of first publication. English editions referred to are those
used in this text.

L'Invitée. Paris: Gallimard, 1943. De Beauvoir's first novel, a fictionalised
account of the 'trio' relationship between herself, Sartre and Olga
Kosakievicz.
(*She Came to Stay*. Harmondsworth: Penguin, 1966.)

Pyrrhus et Cinéas. Paris: Gallimard, 1944. An essay written by de Beauvoir
to explain existentialism to 'the thoughtful reader'. Originally intended as
a 'companion' essay to Sartre's *Being and Nothingness*, it differs from it in
de Beauvoir's emphasis in the distinction between different aspects of
freedom.

Les Bouches inutiles (first performed in 1945). De Beauvoir's only play,
written on the subject of the morality of access to food.

Le Sang des autres. Paris: Gallimard, 1945. The 'Resistance' novel, about
the conflict between personal and social responsibilities.
(*The Blood of Others*. Harmondsworth: Penguin, 1964a.)

Tous les hommes sont mortels. Paris: Gallimard, 1946. A time travelling
novel, in which de Beauvoir attempts to investigate what individuals – in

this case herself and Sartre – are like before and after traumatic events. (*All Men Are Mortal*. Cleveland: World Publishers, 1955.)

Pour une morale de l'ambiguité. Paris: Gallimard, 1948. A philosophical essay written at a time of personal crisis (Sartre's involvement with Dolores) and described by de Beauvoir as 'a frivolous, insignificant thing', the subject is existentialism and again (as in *Pyrrhus and Cinéas*) de Beauvoir's attempt to qualify and define the nature of freedom.
(*The Ethics of Ambiguity*. New York: Philosophical Library, 1967.)

L'Amérique au jour le jour. Paris: Morihien, 1948. A travel book, in which Nelson Algren occasionally appears.
(*America Day by Day*. London: Duckworth, 1952.)

Le Deuxième Sexe. Paris: Gallimard, 1949. De Beauvoir's *magnum opus*, written at Sartre's suggestion and a model for later dichotomising texts on gender relations.
(*The Second Sex*. Toronto: Bantam Books, 1964b.)

'Faut-il-brûler de Sade?', *Les Temps Modernes*, December, 1951 and January, 1952. A defence of the Marquis de Sade, put less in terms of the positive aspects of de Sade and more in terms of the importance of defending the discussion of sexuality.
(*Must We Burn de Sade?* London: Peter Nevill, 1953.)

Les Mandarins. Paris: Gallimard, 1954. De Beauvoir's great novel of post-war French intellectual life. De Beauvoir, Sartre, Camus all appear, as does Algren.
(*The Mandarins*. London: Fontana, 1979a.)

Privilèges. Paris: Gallimard, 1955. Collection of philosophical essays. A collection of three essays, on 'The thought of the right today', 'Merleau-Ponty and Pseudo-Sartrism' and 'Faut-il brûler de Sade?'. The first two were political essays, on French right-wing ideology and on Merleau-Ponty's attack on Sartre's politics.

La Longue Marche. Paris: Gallimard, 1957. An account of de Beauvoir (and Sartre) in China.
(*The Long March*. London: André Deutsch, 1958.)

Mémoires d'une jeune fille rangée. Paris: Gallimard, 1958. The first volume of de Beauvoir's autobiography, which begins in childhood and ends with her meeting with Sartre.

(*Memoirs of a Dutiful Daughter*. Harmondsworth: Penguin, 1959.)

Brigitte Bardot and the Lolita Syndrome. New York: Arno Publishing, 1960. A defence of Brigitte Bardot and *explicit* female sexuality.

La Force de l'age. Paris: Gallimard, 1960. The second volume of auto-biography, from the meeting with Sartre to the end of the Second World War.

(*The Prime of Life*. Harmondsworth: Penguin, 1962a.)

Djamila Boupacha. Paris: Gallimard, 1962. A passionate account of a woman tortured by the French in Algeria.

(*Djamila Boupacha*. London: André Deutsch, 1962b.)

La Force des choses. Paris: Gallimard, 1963. Third volume of autobiography, includes the affair with Algren and the emergence of Sartre and de Beauvoir as public figures.

(*Force of Circumstance*. London: André Deutsch, and Weidenfeld & Nicolson, 1965a.)

Une Mort très douce. Paris: Gallimard, 1964. De Beauvoir's sparse and elegant account of her mother's death.

(*A Very Easy Death*. Harmondsworth: Penguin, 1965b.)

Les Belles Images. Paris: Gallimard, 1966. De Beauvoir's novel of 'consumer' France: includes a move to a new subculture and less autobiographical characters.

(*Les Belles Images*. London: Fontana, 1977.)

La Femme rompue. Paris: Gallimard, 1967. Three novellas, all powerful, about women destroyed by love.

(*The Woman Destroyed*. London: Fontana, 1979b.)

La Vieillesse. Paris: Gallimard, 1970. A socio-economic history of old age which chronicles what de Beauvoir sees as the inevitable debility and alienation of old age. Very much an attempt at an intellectual defence of her own 'old age' (and that of Sartre) de Beauvoir was to express regret about the writing of this book.

(*Old Age*. Harmondsworth: Penguin, 1978.)

Tout compte fait. Paris: Gallimard, 1972. The final version of autobiography includes the meeting with Sylvie le Bon.
(*All Said and Done.* Harmondsworth: Penguin, 1979c.)

Quand prime le spirituel. Paris: Gallimard, 1979. De Beauvoir's first novel, unpublished at the time of writing in the late 1930s.
(*When Things of the Spirit Come First.* London: Fontana, 1983.)

La Cérémonie des adieux suivi de Entretiens avec Jean-Paul Sartre. Paris: Gallimard, 1981. De Beauvoir's farewell, but not her last word, to Sartre.
(*Adieux: Farewell to Sartre.* London: André Deutsch, 1984.)

Letters to Sartre, translated and edited by Quintin Hoare (London: Radius, 1991). A collection of de Beauvoir's letters to Sartre, from 1930 to 1963. The majority of the letters were written during the Second World War, particularly in the period when Sartre was a prisoner of war of the Germans.

Secondary works on Simone de Beauvoir

Algren, Nelson (1965) 'The question of Simone de Beauvoir', *Harpers* (May): 134–6. A less than admiring view of de Beauvoir by an ex-lover.

Appignanesi, Lisa (1988) *Simone de Beauvoir*. Harmondsworth: Penguin.

Ascher, Carol (1981) *Simone de Beauvoir: A Life of Freedom*. Boston: The Beacon Press. An adultory account of de Beauvoir as a 'free' woman and a role model.

Bair, Deidre (1983) 'In summation: the question of conscious feminism or unconscious misogyny in *The Second Sex*', *Simone de Beauvoir Studies*, 1 (1): 56–67. A discussion (by the major biographer of de Beauvoir) of the tensions in de Beauvoir's work between apparent concern for women and contempt for them. The article suggests that the problem is less an issue about de Beauvoir's views on women in general than the issue of de Beauvoir as a woman.

Bair, Deidre (1990) *Simone de Beauvoir*. London: Cape. A richly referenced and fascinating biography, published before later revelations about de Beauvoir.

Bieber, Konrad (1979) *Simone de Beauvoir*. Boston: G.K. Hall.

Butler, Judith (1986) 'Sex and gender in Simone de Beauvoir's *Second Sex*', *Yale French Studies*, 72: 35–49. An article (later developed in the same author's *Gender Trouble*) which argues that de Beauvoir's account of 'becoming' a woman in *The Second Sex* does not necessarily involve a person of female biology.

Carter, Angela (1982) 'The intellectual's Darby and Joan', *New Society* (28 January): 156–7.

Cottrell, Robert (1975) *Simone de Beauvoir*. New York: Frederick Ungar.

132   Simone de Beauvoir

Cranston, Maurice (1978) 'Simone de Beauvoir', in J. Cruickshank (ed.), *The Novelist as Philosopher: Studies in French Fiction, 1935–1960*. Westport, Conn: Greenwood Press.

Crosland, Margaret (1992) *Simone de Beauvoir: The Woman and her Work*. London: Heinemann. A straightforward biography of de Beauvoir, largely dependent on de Beauvoir's autobiography.

Cruickshank, John (1982) 'The limitations of the intellectual', *Times Higher Education Supplement* (26 February): 14.

Cunningham, John (1979) *The Second Sex and Simone de Beauvoir. Guardian* (24 July): 9.

Dietz, Mary (1992) 'Introduction: Debating Simone de Beauvoir', *Signs*, 18 (1): 74–88.

Dijkstra, Sandra (1980) 'Simone de Beauvoir and Betty Friedan: the politics of omission', *Feminist Studies*, 6 (2): 290–303.

Doeuff, Michèle le (1980) 'Simone de Beauvoir and existentialism', *Feminist Studies*, 6 (2): 227–89. A sophisticated account of de Beauvoir's interpretation of, and contribution to, existentialism by a leading French philosopher.

Doeuff, Michèle le (1987) 'Operative philosophy: Simone de Beauvoir and Existentialism', in Elaine Marks (ed.), *Critical Essays on Simone de Beauvoir*. Boston: Hall. pp. 144–54.

Evans, Mary (1980) 'Views of women and men in the work of Simone de Beauvoir', *Women's Studies International Quarterly*, 3: 395–404. An essay which sets out an account of the male and female in de Beauvoir's work; essentially, the male is the centre of the universe and women peripheral.

Evans, Mary (1983) 'Simone de Beauvoir: dilemmas of a feminist radical'. In Dale Spender (ed.), *Feminist Theorists*. London: The Women's Press. The 'dilemma' in this article being that of how de Beauvoir proposes women can ever emancipate themselves, given that their only positive image is that of masculinity.

Evans, Mary (1985) *Simone de Beauvoir: A Feminist Mandarin*. London: Tavistock. A biographical study of de Beauvoir written before the publication of additional biographical works about de Beauvoir, and in a personal/political context which maintained clearer distinctions, particularly around issues relating to gender difference.

Felstiner, Mary Lowenthal (1980) 'Seeing *The Second Sex* through the second wave', *Feminist Studies*, 6 (2) (Summer): 249–76.

Forster, Penny and Sutton, Imogen (eds) (1989) *Daughters of de Beauvoir*. London: The Women's Press.

Fuchs, Jo-Ann (1980) 'Female eroticism in *The Second Sex*', *Feminist Studies*, 6 (2) (Summer): 304–13.

Fullbrook, Kate and Fullbrook, Edward (1993) *Simone de Beauvoir and Jean-Paul Sartre: The Remaking of a Twentieth Century Legend*. Hemel Hempstead: Harvester Wheatsheaf. An interesting re-evaluation of de Beauvoir's contribution to Sartre's work, which suggests that de Beauvoir's contribution was both more crucial and more critical than is sometimes supposed.

Gerassi, John (1976) 'Interview with Simone de Beauvoir', *Society* (January/February): 79–85. An interesting interview, not least because John

Gerassi is the son of de Beauvoir's friend Stépha. In it, de Beauvoir asserts that all feminists are by definition 'Leftist'.

Hardwick, Elizabeth (1953) 'The subjection of women', *Partisan Review*, 20 (3): 321–31.

Heath, Jane (1989) *Simone de Beauvoir*. Brighton: Harvester. A thoughtful account of de Beauvoir, which illustrates the rereading of de Beauvoir by feminists. Heath takes a critical view of de Beauvoir, in particular her refusal to identify herself as a woman and with 'the feminine'.

Jardine, Alice (1979) 'Interview with Simone de Beauvoir', *Signs*, 5 (2) (Winter): 224–36. An interview which contains useful material on de Beauvoir's views on gender and writing: specifically, she appears to reject the idea of a 'feminine' writing as suggested by Hélène Cixous.

Jeanson, Francis (1966) *Simone de Beauvoir ou l'entreprise de vivre*. Paris: Editions du Seuil. A sympathetic interpretation.

Johnson, Douglas (1981) 'La Grande Sartreuse', *London Review of Books* (15 October–4 November): 20–1.

Kaufmann-McCall, Dorothy (1979) 'Simone de Beauvoir, *The Second Sex* and Jean-Paul Sartre', *Signs*, 5 (2) (Winter): 209–23.

Keefe, Terry (1983) *Simone de Beauvoir: Study of her Writings*. London: Harrap.

Keefe, Terry (1993) 'The flawed bible', *Times Higher Education Supplement*, 26 March: 19.

Kruks, Sonia (1992) 'Gender and subjectivity: Simone de Beauvoir and contemporary feminism', *Signs*, 18 (1): 89–110.

Leighton, Jean (1975) *Simone de Beauvoir on Women*. London: Associated University Presses.

Lloyd, Genevieve (1983) 'Masters, slaves and others', *Radical Philosophy*, 34 (Summer): 2–9.

Madsen, Axel (1977) *Hearts and Minds: The Common Journey of Simone de Beauvoir and Jean-Paul Sartre*. New York: Morrow.

Marks, Elaine (1973) *Simone de Beauvoir: Encounter with Death*. New Brunswick, NJ: Rutgers University Press. The main argument is that de Beauvoir is obsessed with death, yet cannot confront it.

Marks, Elaine (ed.) (1987) *Critical Essays on Simone de Beauvoir*. Boston: Hall. As the title suggests (and as was the case in Elaine Marks's earlier work) the essays here tend to a critical reading of de Beauvoir.

Moi, Toril (1990) *Feminist Theory and Simone de Beauvoir*. Oxford: Blackwell. An outline of the arguments to be developed by the same author in *Simone de Beauvoir: The Making of an Intellectual Woman*, namely that de Beauvoir has suffered attack by a culture which cannot allow female intellectuals.

Moi, Toril (1994) *Simone de Beauvoir: The Making of an Intellectual Woman*. Oxford, Blackwell. A further development of the argument above and a passionate defence of de Beauvoir's life and work in the face of often furious criticism.

Moorehead, Caroline (1974) 'A talk with Simone de Beauvoir', *New York Times Magazine*, (2 June): 16–34.

O'Brien, Mary (1981) *The Politics of Reproduction*. London: Routledge & Kegan Paul.

Radford, C.B. (1965) 'The Authenticity of Simone de Beauvoir', *Nottingham French Studies*, IV (2) (October): 91–104.

Radford, C.B. (1967–68) 'Simone de Beauvoir: feminism's friend or foe? Part I', *Nottingham French Studies*, VI (2) (October): 87–102; Part II. *Nottingham French Studies*, VII (1) (May): 39–53.

Schwarzer, Alice (1984) *Simone de Beauvoir Today: Conversations 1972–1982*. London: Chatto & Windus, The Hogarth Press.

Simone de Beauvoir Society (1983) 'Simone de Beauvoir and women', *Simone de Beauvoir Studies*, 1 (1) (Fall): 1–24. A sympathetic account of de Beauvoir's views on women, in a publication of a loyal support group in the United States.

Simons, Margaret A. (1983) 'The silencing of Simone de Beauvoir: guess what's missing from *The Second Sex*', *Women's Studies International Forum*, 6 (5): 559–64. Extremely useful textual analysis of the English (H.M. Parshley) translation of *The Second Sex*, which demonstrates that a great deal was art *or* mistranslated from the French edition.

Simons, Margaret and Benjamin, J. (1979) 'Simone de Beauvoir: an interview', *Feminist Studies*, 5 (2) (Summer): 330–45.

Walters, Margaret (1976) 'The rights and wrongs of women: Mary Wollstonecraft, Harriet Martineau and Simone de Beauvoir', in Ann Oakley and Juliet Mitchell (eds), *The Rights and Wrongs of Women*. Harmondsworth: Penguin. One of the most insightful, if brief, essays on de Beauvoir ever written, which maintains a considerable critical independence about her.

Whitmarsh, Anne (1981) *Simone de Beauvoir and the Limits of Commitment*. Cambridge: Cambridge University Press.

Yale French Studies (1986) vol. 72, Special Issue on de Beauvoir. Contains essays by (among others) Judith Butler and Elaine Marks. The latter's essay 'Transgressing the (in)cont(in)ent boundaries: the body in decline' is a particularly energetic discussion of de Beauvoir's alleged fear of mortality.

Zéphir, Pierre (1982) *Le Néo-Feminisme de Simone de Beauvoir*. Paris: Denoel Gonthier.

Other works

Adorno, T.W., Frenkel-Brunswik, Else, Levinson, Daniel and Sanford, R. (1969) *The Authoritarian Personality*. New York: Norton.

Aronson, Ronald (1980) *Jean-Paul Sartre: Philosophy in the World*. London: George Allen & Unwin.

Barrett, Michèle (1980) *Women's Oppression Today*. London: Verso.

Brenner, Johanna and Ramas, Maria (1984) 'Rethinking women's oppression', *New Left Review* (March/April), 144: 33–7.

Brombert, V. (1960) *The Intellectual Hero*. Philadelphia and New York: J.P. Lippincott.

Butler, Judith (1990) *Gender Trouble*. London: Routledge.

Caws, Peter (1979) *Sartre*. London: Routledge & Kegan Paul.

Charlesworth, Max (1975) *The Existentialists and Jean-Paul Sartre*. Queensland: University of Queensland Press.

Chodorow, Nancy (1978) *The Reproduction of Mothering*. Berkeley: University of California Press.

Cohen-Solal, Annie (1987) *Sartre: A Life*. London: Heinemann.

Coward, Rosalind (1983) *Patriarchal Precedents: Sexuality and Social Relations*. London: Routledge and Kegan Paul.

Delphy, Christine (1977) *The Main Enemy*. London: Women's Research and Resources Centre Pamphlet.

Donohue, H.E.F. (1963) *Conversations with Nelson Algren*. New York: Hill and Wang.

Engels, Frederick (1985) *The Origin of the Family, Private Property and the State*. Harmondsworth: Penguin.

Firestone, Shulamith (1971) *A Dialectic of Sex*. New York: Bantam Books.

Fraser, Nancy and Bartky, Sandra (eds) (1992) *Re-evaluating French Feminism: Critical Essays on Difference, Agency, Culture*. Bloomington: Indiana University Press.

Gilligan, Carol (1983) *In a Different Voice*. Cambridge, Mass: Harvard University Press.

Goldmann, Lucien (1970) *Power and Humanism*. Nottingham: Bertrand Russell Peace Foundation.

Gunew, Sneja (1990) *Feminist Knowledge: Critique and Construct*. London: Routledge.

Hayman, Ronald (1987) *Sartre: A Biography*. New York: Simon & Schuster.

Hughes, H. Stuart (1968) *The Obstructed Path: French Social Thought in the Years of Desperation, 1930–1960*. New York: Harper & Row.

Humphries, Jane (1981) 'Protective legislation, the capitalist state and working class men: the case of the 1842 Mines Regulation Act', *Feminist Review*, 7: 1–33.

Johnson, R.W. (1981) *The Long March of the French Left*. London: Macmillan.

Kaplan, Cora (1979) 'Radical feminism and literature', *Red Letters*, 9: 4–16.

Kaplan, Louise (1991) *Female Perversions*. Harmondsworth: Penguin.

Kaufmann-McCall, Dorothy (1983) 'Politics of difference: the women's movement in France from May 1968 to Mitterrand', *Signs*, 9 (2): 282–93.

Lorde, Audré (1984) *Sister Outsider*. Trumansberg: Crossing Press.

Macey, David (1994) *The Lives of Michel Foucault*. London: Vintage.

Macmillan, James (1981) *Housewife or Harlot? The Place of Women in French Society, 1870–1940*. New York: St Martin's Press.

Marks, Elaine and Courtivron, Isabelle de (1981) *New French Feminisms*. Brighton: Harvester.

May, Elaine Tyler (1980) *Great Expectations*. Chicago: University of Chicago Press.

Meszaros, Istvan (1979) *The Work of Sartre: Volume 1, The Search for Freedom*. Brighton: Harvester.

Miller, Jean Baker (1979) *Towards a New Psychology of Women*. Harmondsworth: Penguin.

Millett, Kate (1971) *Sexual Politics*. London: Virago.

Mitchell, Juliet (1975) *Psychoanalysis and Feminism*. Harmondsworth: Penguin.

Moi, Toril (1982) 'Jealousy and sexual difference', *Feminist Review*, 11 (Summer): 53–68.

Plath, Sylvia (1966) *The Bell Jar*. London: Faber & Faber.

Plath, Sylvia (1982) *The Journals of Sylvia Plath*. New York: The Dial Press.

Rich, Adrienne (1978) *Dream of a Common Language: Poems 1974–1977*. New York: W.W. Norton.

Rich, Adrienne (1979) *Of Woman Born*. London: Virago. First published 1976.

Rowbotham, Sheila (1973) *Hidden from History*. London: Pluto.

Sartre, Jean-Paul (1948) *Existentialism and Humanism*. London: Methuen. First published 1946 as *L'existentialisme est un humanisme*, Paris: Nagel.

Sartre, Jean-Paul (1952) *The Communists and the Peace*. New York: Braziller, 1968.

Sartre, Jean-Paul (1956) *Being and Nothingness*. New York: Philosophical Library. First published 1940 as *L'Etre et Le néant*, Paris: Gallimard.

Sartre, Jean-Paul (1959) *The Age of Reason*. New York: Bantam. First published 1945 as *L'Age de Raison*, Paris: Gallimard.

Sartre, Jean-Paul (1963) *Saint Genet*. New York: New American Library. First published 1952 as *Saint Genet*, Paris: Gallimard.

Sartre, Jean-Paul (1964a) *Nausea*. New York: New Directions. First published 1938 as *La Nausée*, Paris: Gallimard.

Sartre, Jean-Paul (1964b) *Words*. New York: Braziller. First published 1964 as *Les Mots*, Paris: Gallimard.

Sartre, Jean-Paul (1968) *The Communists and the Peace*. New York: Braziller. First published 1952 as *Les Communistes et la Paix*, Paris: Gallimard.

Sartre, Jean-Paul (1976) *The Critique of Dialectical Reason*. London: New Left Books. First published 1966 as *Critique de la raison dialectique*, Paris: Gallimard.

Sartre, Jean-Paul (1977) *Life/Situations: Essays Written and Spoken*. New York: Pantheon.

Sartre, Jean-Paul (1981) *The Family Idiot: Gustave Flaubert*. Chicago: University of Chicago Press. First published 1971 as *L'Idiot de la famille*, Paris: Gallimard.

Sartre, Jean-Paul (1983) *Cahiers pour une morale*. Paris: Gallimard.

Sartre, Jean-Paul (1992a) *Witness to My Life*. London: Hamish Hamilton. First published 1983 as *Lettres au Castor et à quelques autres*, Paris: Gallimard.

Sartre, Jean-Paul (1992b) *Witness to My Life: The Letters of Jean-Paul Sartre to Simone de Beauvoir, 1926–1939*, edited by Simone de Beauvoir. London: Hamish Hamilton.

Sartre, Jean-Paul (1993) *Quiet Moments in a War*. Harmondsworth: Penguin.

Sartre, Jean-Paul (1994) *Quiet Moments in a War*. London: Hamish Hamilton. First published 1983 as *Les Carnets de la drôle de guerre*, Paris: Gallimard.

Sayers, Janet (1982) *Biological Politics*. London: Tavistock.

Sayers, Janet (1985) *Sexual Contradictions*. London: Routledge.

Shaktini, Namascar (1982) 'Displacing the phallic subject: Wittig's lesbian writing', *Signs*, 8 (1) (Autumn): 29–44.

Signs (1981) Special Issue on French Feminist Theory, 7 (1) (Autumn).

Thompson, E.P. (1977) *Whigs and Hunters*. Harmondsworth: Peregrine.

Walkowitz, Judith (1980) *Prostitution and Victorian Society: Women, Class and the State*. Cambridge: Cambridge University Press.

Weeks, Jeffrey (1981) *Sex, Politics and Society*. London: Longman.

Wilson, Sarah (1993) 'Paris post war: in search of the absolute', in Frances Morris (ed.), *Paris Post War: Art and Existentialism, 1945–55*. London: Tate Gallery.

Zaretsky, Eli (1976) *Capitalism, The Family and Personal Life*. London: Pluto Press.

Zerilli, Linda (1992) 'Beauvoir and Kristeva on Maternity', *Signs*, 18 (1) (Autumn): 111–35.

Index

academia, and sexual politics of 1960s,
    10
Adieux: A Farewell to Sartre, 72, 81–2,
    96, 101, 124
adolescence, SdB's views on
        dependency in, 55–6
adoption
    of Arlette Elkaïm by Sartre, 29, 72, 95
    of Sylvie le Bon by SdB, 29
Algeria, action over French policy in,
    28, 71, 116
Algren, Nelson
    influences on SdB's work, 62–3
    public acknowledgement and
            portrayal in *The Mandarins*, 28,
            37–8, 59–60
    SdB's relationship with, 37, 44,
            59–60, 61, 76, 106
All Men are Mortal, 36
All Said and Done, 73, 75, 80–1, 91,
    117, 124
America Day by Day, 126
Arlette *see* Elkaïm
Aury, Dominique, 113–14
autobiography of SdB, 80, 91–3, 110–11
    comparison with Sartre's, 41–2, 97
    interpretation of, 92–3, 116–18
    selective nature of, 29, 85, 93

Badinter, Elisabeth, 110
Bair, Deidre, 18, 59, 73, 80, 83, 105–6,
    110
    SdB's control of biography by, 29,
            88–9
Beauvoir, Françoise de (mother)
    death of, 12, 19, 80, 83, 117–18
    family and domestic life, 16, 17, 120
    influence on SdB, 8, 49, 57, 68–9
    moral and religious values, 17, 18,
            19, 68
    political understanding, 67–8
    relationship with daughters, 17, 18,
            19, 98
    relationship with Georges, 8, 19–20,
            21, 49, 57, 69–70, 89
    SdB's attempts to please, 20
    SdB's determination to be different
            from, 11–12, 13
Beauvoir, Georges de (father)
    attitudes to politics, 67, 68
    attitudes to religion, 17, 68
    family life, 15, 17
    influence on SdB, 19, 49, 103
    relationship with Françoise, 8,
            19–20, 21, 49, 57, 69–70, 89
    SdB's attempts to please, 20–1, 102
Beauvoir, Hélène de (sister), 16, 17, 99

Beauvoir, Simone de
  adolescence, 18–19, 20–1
  autobiography *see* autobiography of
      SdB
  biographies of, 29, 30, 88–9, 119
  contemporary readings of, 12–13,
      35, 38, 49, 54–5
  desire for independence and
      emancipation, 3–4, 57, 69, 88
  as 'different', 6–7, 11, 13, 91, 109,
      125, 127
  early family life and social
      background, 14, 15–20, 67–8
  fame and status as public figure,
      27–8, 71, 115, 116
  final years and death of, 84
  friendships and attitudes to others,
      20, 75, 98–100
  intellectual contribution compared
      to Sartre, 48–51, 70–1, 124
  involvement with feminism *see*
      feminism
  involvement in intellectual life, 110–11
  involvement in politics, 5, 28, 67, 71,
      78–9, 115–16
  need for central intimate 'other', 8,
      74–6, 78
  organising world view, 74, 117–18
  rational and determined nature of,
      18–19, 69, 72, 120
  relationship with Algren *see* Algren,
      Nelson
  relationship with parents *see*
      Beauvoir, Françoise de;
      Beauvoir, Georges de
  relationship with Sartre *see* Sartre,
      Jean-Paul
  relationship with Sylvie le Bon, 29,
      42, 75, 80, 109
  relationships with women, 59, 60–1,
      75, 76, 80, 109
  social context of life, 4–5, 12
  writing compared to Sartre's, 102–3
  writing motivated by emotional life
      and loss, 8, 26–7, 102

Beauvoir, Sylvie le Bon de *see* le Bon,
      Sylvie
Being and Nothingness, 51
Blood of Others, The, 33, 36–7
body
  reference in *She Came to Stay* to,
      50–1
  SdB's relationship to own, 21, 25
Bost, Jaques, 99
Butler, Judith, 34, 61–2

Camus, Albert, 99
Communist Party, 115–16
contraception, 54, 59
culture, women's relationship to,
      112–13, 119

death
  relationship with central other as
      SdB's protection from, 75, 77
  of SdB's mother, 12, 19, 80, 83,
      117–18
Dolores *see* Vanetti
domestic sphere *see* public and private
      spheres

education
  SdB's attempts to please father, 20,
      21, 102
  SdB's success in, 21–2, 120–1
  SdB's time at the Sorbonne, 23
Elkaïm, Arlette, 42, 82, 95–6
  adoption by Sartre, 29, 72, 95
emancipation of women, SdB's desire
      for, 3–4, 57, 69, 88
Ethics of Ambiguity, The, 32
existentialism
  and origins of *The Second Sex*, 48
  SdB's contribution to theory of, 124

family, 'The Family', 99, 107
family life of SdB, 14, 15–20
  influence on SdB, 49, 57
  parental relationship, 8, 19–20, 21,
      49, 57, 69–70, 89

political affiliations in, 67–8
religious and moral values in, 17–18, 68
social background, 15–17
female introvert, SdB accused of being, 24–5, 56
femininity
and masculinity in *The Second Sex*, 34, 52–3, 62–4, 121–3
of SdB's autobiography, 42
SdB's refusal of, 35–7, 40
feminism
1960s and 1970s rise of, 111–12
as challenge to SdB's life-pattern, 74
changing nature of, 2
and nature of politics, 68, 71–2
and public and private spheres, 66, 74
rediscovery of SdB as problematic for, 64, 108, 111–15, 120–7
SdB's influence and status as 'mother' of, 1, 2, 11–13, 65, 110, 119
SdB's involvement with and understanding of, 39, 40, 72–3, 87, 107, 108–9
theories of language, 45, 109
understanding of knowledge, 58
views of SdB, 118–19
Force of Circumstance, 39, 40, 91, 115, 116, 117
Foucault, Michel, 5, 110
Freud, S., 77–8
SdB's views of psychoanalysis and, 35–6, 54
Fullbrook, Kate and Edward, 50–1

gender
and sex in *The Second Sex*, 34, 61–4
see also femininity; masculinity
Giacometti, Alberto, 113, 114

Heath, Jane, 35
heterosexuality, SdB's understanding of, 34, 36, 37, 38, 59–60, 62–3, 103–4

housewife, SdB accused of being, 25, 56
human nature, SdB's views of, 121–2

intellect, role in Sartre's relationship with SdB, 27, 42–3, 44, 97–8
intellectual, SdB as, 23, 24, 125–6
intellectual ideas, gendered origin and ownership of, 48–9, 51
intellectual life
contribution and standing of Sartre and SdB, 48–51, 70–1, 123–4
gendered nature of, 57–8
Sartre and SdB as 'legendary couple' in, 28
Sartre's involvement in, 107, 111
SdB's involvement in, 23, 110–11
shifting nature of, 108
Irigaray, Luce, 45

Kaplan, Louise, 77–8
knowledge
changing ideas and advances in, 4–5
relationship of women to, 57–8, 125–6
Sartre's search for universal theory of, 32
SdB's commitment to objective, 10
SdB's view of universal nature of, 32, 58, 62, 121
Kosakievicz, Olga, 24, 26, 44, 49, 99, 100–1, 105
Kosakievicz, Wanda, 76, 99, 105
Kruks, Sonia, 33–4

language
Sartre's and SdB's use of, 97–8, 101
SdB's views on, 45, 109
Lanzmann, Claude, 28–9, 99
laws, SdB's and Sartre's belief in universal, 22
le Bon, Sylvie (later le Bon de Beauvoir), 42, 75, 80, 109
adoption by SdB, 29
le Coin, Elisabeth (ZaZa), 15, 20, 21, 103
Leduc, Violette, 99

Les Temps Modernes, 84–5
lesbianism, SdB's writings on and
     attitudes toward, 36, 60, 109
Lévy, Benny, 42, 72, 82, 96
literature, used as evidence of social
     attitudes, 55
Long March, The, 126
Lorde, Audré, 121
loss, and emotion as motivation for
     writing, 8, 26–7, 102

'M' *see* Vanetti, Dolores
Mandarins, The, 37–8, 59–60, 63
Maoism, Sartre's involvement with, 45,
     72, 107
Marks, Elaine, 74–5
marriage, SdB's views on, 56, 57
masculinity
   and femininity in *The Second Sex*, 34,
        52–3, 62–4, 121–3
   Sartre as representative of SdB's, 78,
        79
   and SdB's attraction to Sartre, 75, 92
   SdB's bias toward, 36, 40, 113–15,
        121–2
   SdB's lessening concern with, 43
   SdB's understanding of, 34, 103–4
maternity *see* motherhood
Memoirs of a Dutiful Daughter, 8, 14,
     15, 19, 40, 57, 91, 116
misogyny
   Sartre's, 45
   SdB's discussion in *The Second Sex*
        of, 52, 55
modernity, context of SdB's and
     Sartre's work, 22, 44–5
Moi, Toril, 64, 89–90, 120
moral values, and SdB's early life,
     17–19, 68
motherhood, SdB's views on, 11–12,
     54, 57, 123
mother
   Sartre's relationship with his, 98–9,
        101, 102
   SdB's *see* Beauvoir, Françoise de

Olga *see* Kosakievicz, Olga
others
   as central theme in SdB's work, 51
   Sartre's and SdB's relationships with
        see Beauvoir, Simone de; Sartre,
        Jean-Paul
   SdB's need for central intimate
        other, 8, 74–6, 78
   'The Family', 99, 107
   women as, 48, 51–2, 53–4, 119

philosophy
   existentialism, 48, 124
   SdB's background in and
        understanding of, 32–3, 58, 121
   SdB's contribution to, 123–4
   She Came to Stay as philosophical
        treatise, 50–1
Plath, Sylvia, 115
politics
   changing nature after 1968 of, 44
   of interpersonal relationships, 5–6
   nature of, 68, 71–2
   Sartre's involvement in, 28, 71, 78–9,
        115–16
   and SdB's family background,
        67–8
   SdB's involvement in, 5, 28, 67, 71,
        78–9, 115–16
   and women, 68
postmodernism, 58
Prime of Life, The, 23, 56, 91, 100, 114,
     116–17, 120
psychoanalytic theory
   SdB's views of, 10, 35–6, 54
   used to understand SdB, 77–8, 92
public and private spheres
   and changing relationship between
        SdB and Sartre, 72, 85
   feminist understanding of, 67, 74
   and interpretations of SdB's
        autobiography, 116–18
   Sartre as representative of SdB's
        public sphere, 75–6, 78–9, 81,
        118

SdB's writing and understanding of, 16, 52, 66–7, 119–20

Ray, Evelyne, 106
reality
    consideration in *She Came to Stay* of, 51
    Sartre's construction of own, 97, 101
relationships
    between sexes, 52–3
    politics of interpersonal, 5–6
    see also Beauvoir, Simone de; Sartre, Jean-Paul
religion
    SdB's attitudes to, 17, 20, 80–1
    SdB's family background, 17–18, 68
Richier, Germaine, 113–14
Rowbotham, Sheila, 111–12

Sarraute, Nathalie, 113, 114
Sartre, Jean-Paul
    attitudes to women, 41, 45, 47–8, 96–7, 101–2
    autobiography, 41–2, 97
    childhood, 97, 101–2
    construction of own reality, 97, 101
    deconstruction of own work, 82
    fame and participation in intellectual life, 27–8, 107, 111
    final years and death of, 81–4, 95–6
    intellectual contribution compared to SdB, 48–51, 70–1, 124
    involvement with Maoism, 45, 72, 107
    letters to and from SdB, 22, 27, 76–7, 94
    political activity, 28, 71, 78–9, 115–16
    recorded interviews with SdB, 72, 96–7, 101
    relationship with SdB
        crisis in, 24–6
        intellectual nature of, 27, 42–3, 44, 97–8
        interpretations of, 7, 9, 88–91, 118–19

nature of, 7, 9, 22–9, 70, 75–9, 83, 124–5
    responses to SdB's relationships with others, 42, 106–7
    Sartre as central figure in SdB's life, 13, 88–9, 92, 93, 95, 107–8, 124–5
    Sartre as representative of public sphere for SdB, 75–6, 78–9, 81, 118
    Sartre's influences on SdB's work, 7–8, 9, 24, 62–3, 124–5
    SdB's attempts to please, 25, 56, 79
    SdB's organisation of other relationships, 104–6
    SdB's shift away in final years from, 79–80, 81, 82–3, 90
    SdB's support and involvement in work of, 93–4, 122
    relationship with Arlette Elkaïm, 29, 42, 72, 82, 95–6
    relationship with Olga Kosakievicz, 24, 26, 44, 49, 99, 100–1, 105
    relationship with Wanda Kosakievicz, 76, 99, 105
    relationship with Benny Lévy, 42, 72, 82, 96
    relationship with parents, 98–9, 101–2
    relationship with Dolores Vanetti (alias 'M'), 44, 47, 74, 77, 92, 105
    relationship with Michelle Vian, 99, 105–6
    SdB's responses to others' relationships with, 24, 26, 41–2, 93, 94–6, 100–1, 104–6, 124–5
    SdB's writings about, 41, 42, 89
    theoretical and political differences with SdB, 31–4, 45, 71–2, 84–5
    writing compared to SdB's, 102–3
    writings about SdB, 42
Sayers, Janet, 77

Second Sex, The
  biographical experiences in, 56–7,
      62–3
  importance to feminism, 119
  interpretation and problematic
      nature for feminism of, 33–5, 40,
      73–4, 121–2
  origins and context of writing, 47–8,
      59
  sex and gender in, 34, 61–4
  subtext of heterosexual desire in, 60
  themes of, 51–8
  women as 'the other', 51–2, 53–4
sex, and gender in *The Second Sex*, 34,
      61–4
sexuality
  SdB's feelings of own, 21, 23, 25–6,
      35, 37, 39, 59–60, 109
  SdB's understanding of
      heterosexuality, 34, 36, 37, 38,
      59–60, 62–3, 103–4
  SdB's understanding of women's
      lives and, 54
  SdB's writings on and attitudes
      toward lesbianism, 36, 60, 109
  see also femininity; masculinity
She Came to Stay, 24, 36, 38, 49–51
social class, SdB's background and,
      14–17
social world
  SdB's experiences of, 3–6
  SdB's and Sartre's stable and
      ordered, 24
  see also intellectual life
Sylvie *see* le Bon, Sylvie

teaching, 20, 24

universalism
  and context of SdB's writing, 22, 35
  SdB's views of, 32, 58, 62, 121

Vanetti, Dolores (alias 'M'), 44, 74, 77,
      92, 105
Very Easy Death, A, 19, 68–9, 117–18,
      125
Vian, Michelle, 99, 105–6

Walters, Margaret, 121–2
Wanda *see* Kosakievicz, Wanda
Wilson, Sarah, 113–14
Witness to My Life, 22
Woman Destroyed, The, 45
women
  and politics, 68
  relationship to culture, 112–13, 119
  relationship to knowledge, 57–8,
      125–6
  Sartre's attitudes to, 41, 45, 47–8,
      96–7, 101–2
  SdB's attitudes to and
      understanding of, 1, 23, 33–4,
      39–40, 104
  SdB's 'difference' from, 91, 109, 125,
      127
  SdB's increasing concern with, 43,
      45
  SdB's neglect in writings of, 113–15
  SdB's views of independence and
      dependency of, 8, 33–4, 38–9,
      55–6
    as 'the other', 48, 51–2, 53–4, 119

ZaZa *see* le Coin, Elisabeth
Zerilli, Linda, 123